FINGERPICKING GUITAR BIBLE

AUTHENTIC TRANSCRIPTIONS
WITH NOTES AND TABLATURE

ISBN 978-1-4234-9429-4

HAL•LEONARD®
CORPORATION

7777 W. BLUEMOUND RD. P.O. BOX 13819 MILWAUKEE, WI 53213

Visit Hal Leonard Online at
www.halleonard.com

from John Fahey - *America*

America

Written by John Fahey

Drop D tuning:
(low to high) D-A-D-G-B-E

Rubato ♩ = approx. 180
* G6

Gtr. 1
(12-str. acous.)

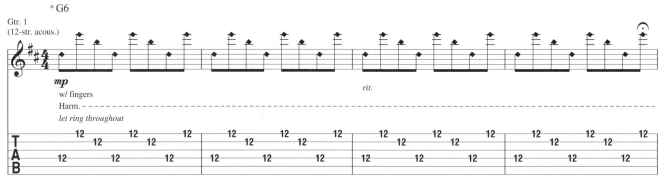

*Chord symbols reflect implied harmony.

A tempo
D6

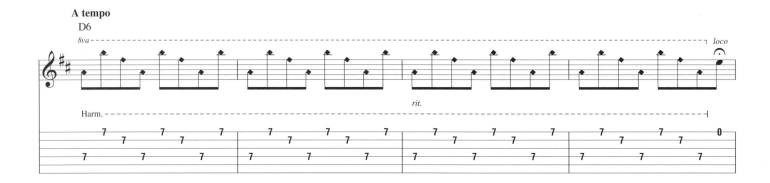

A tempo
G6

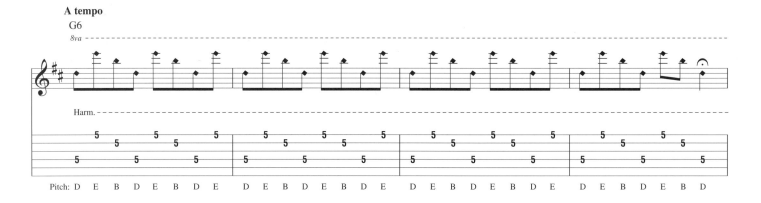

♩ = approx. 100
B6   G6   D6

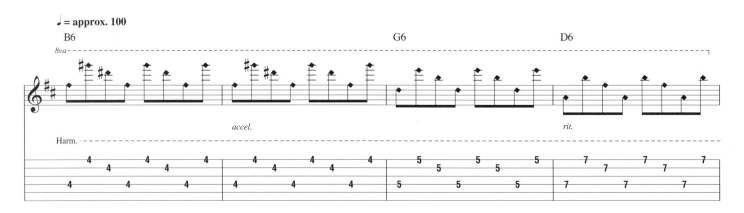

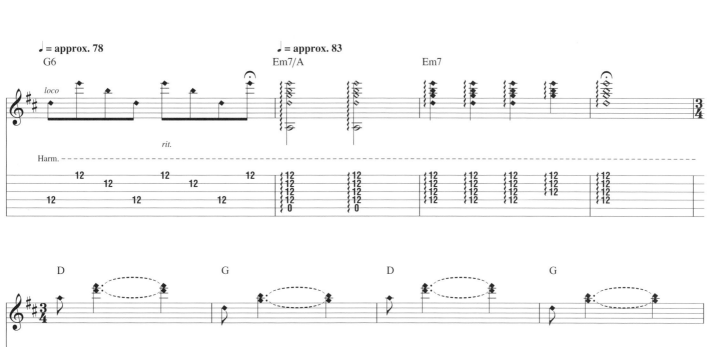

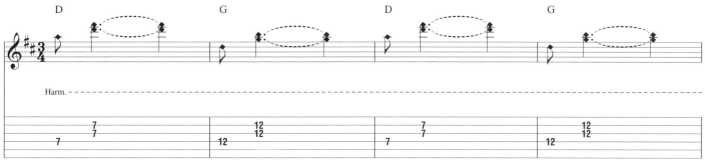

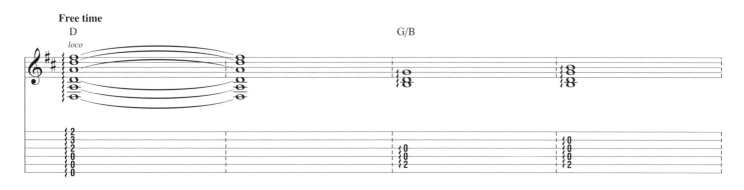

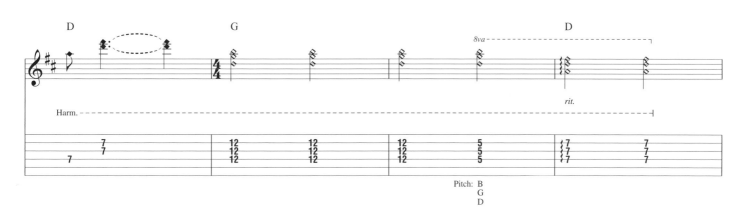

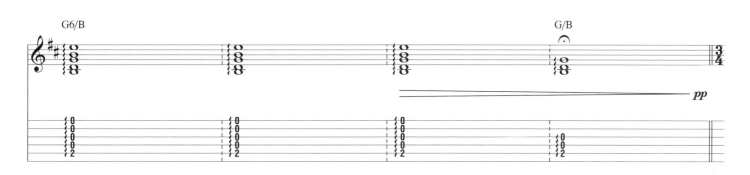

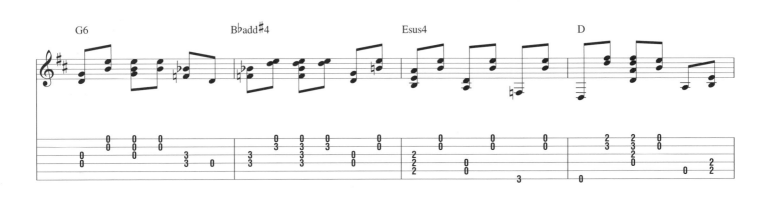

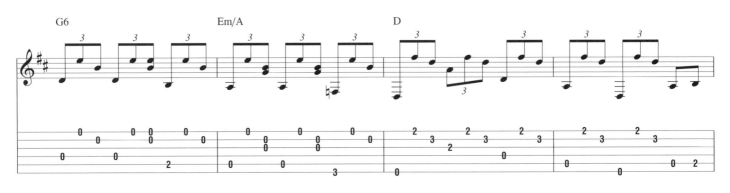

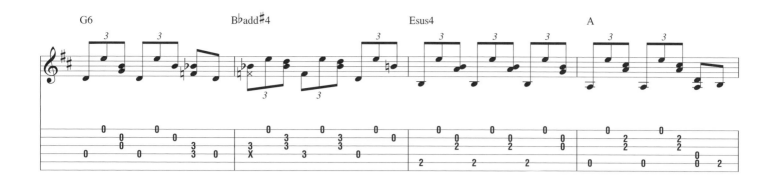

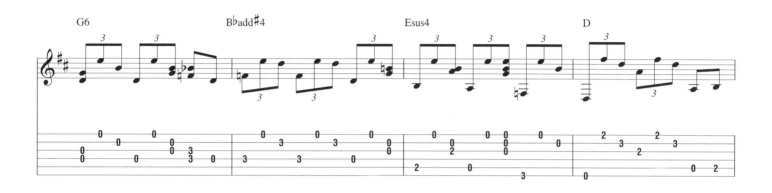

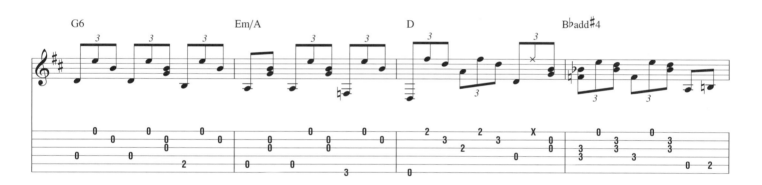

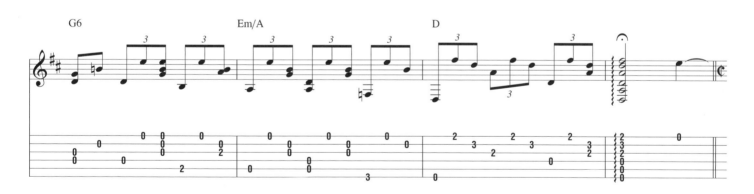

C

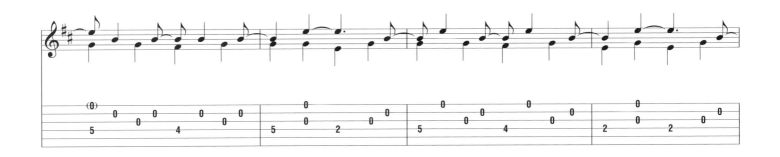

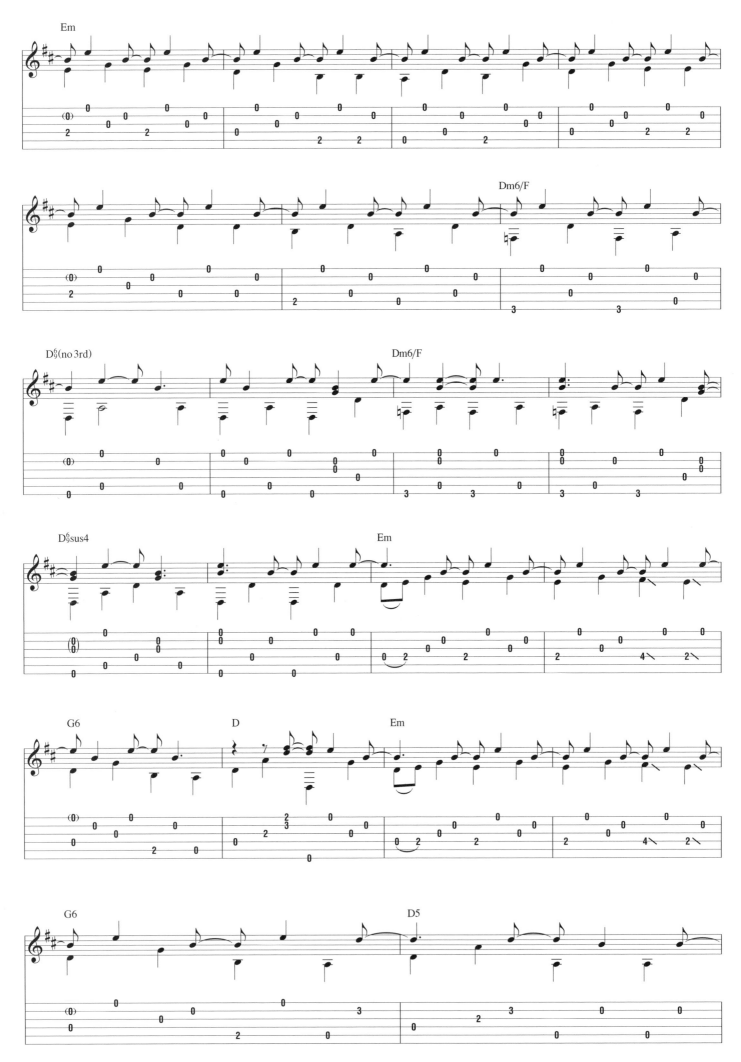

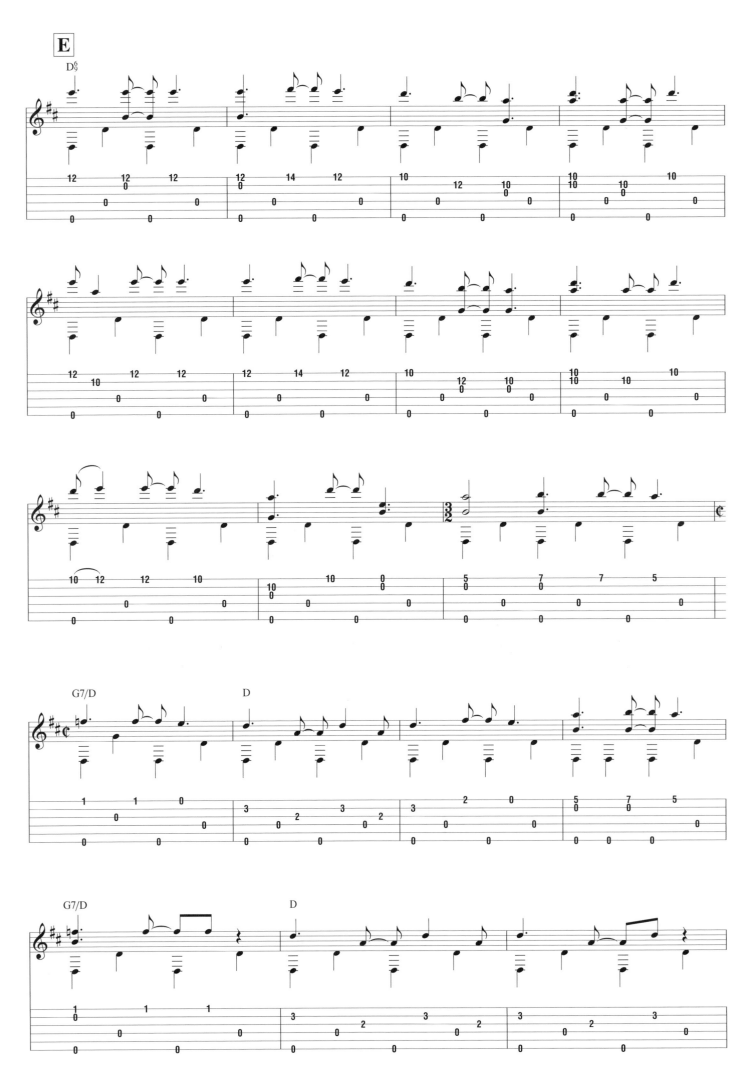

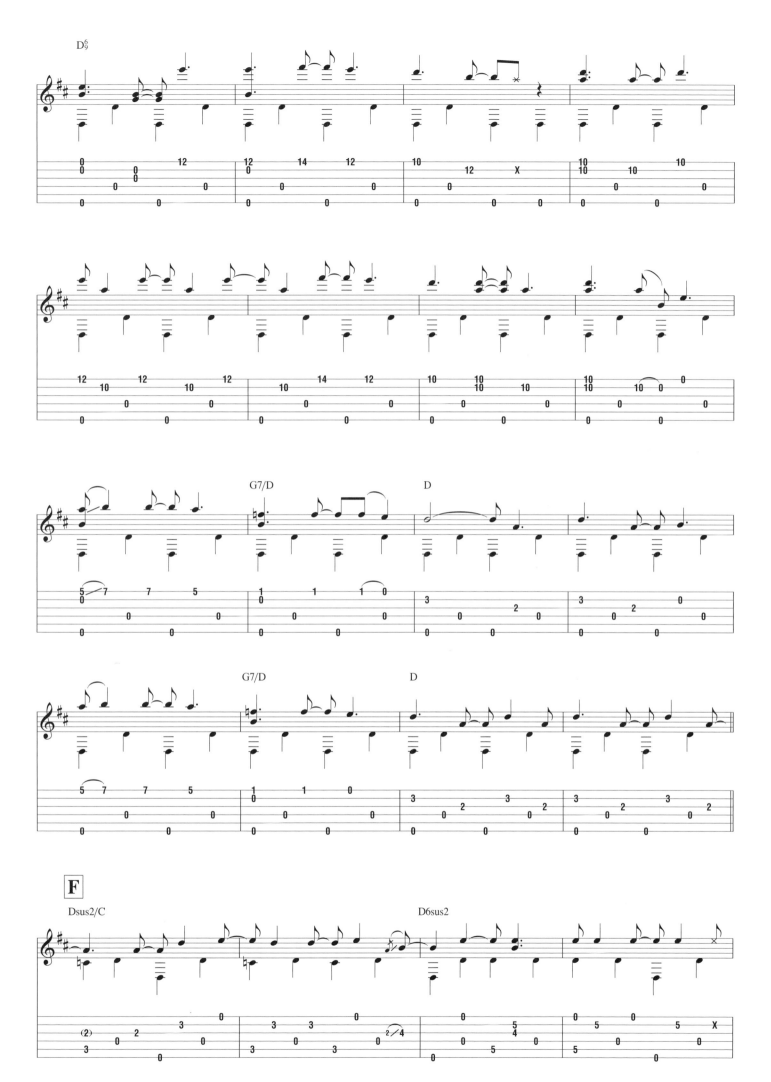

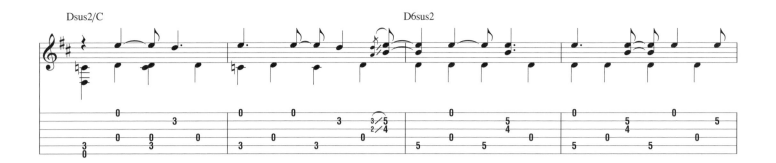

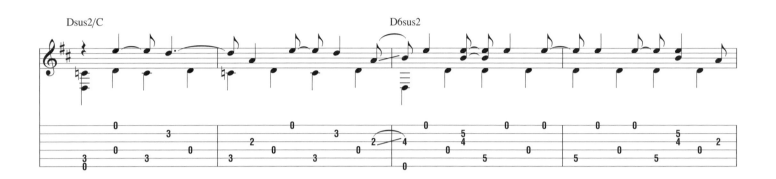

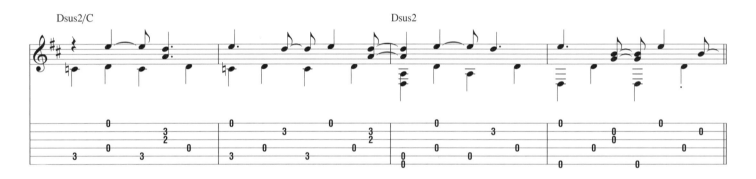

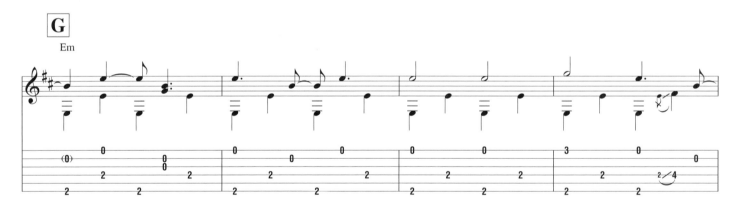

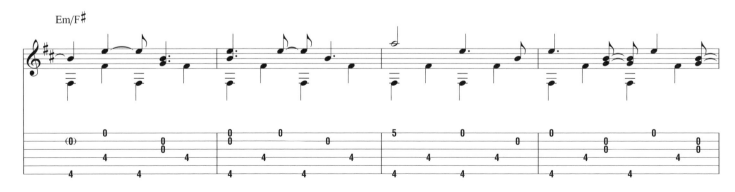

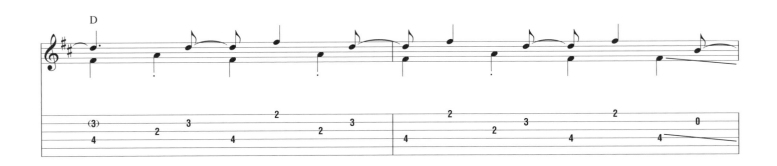

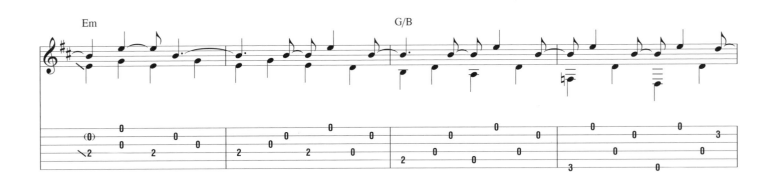

15

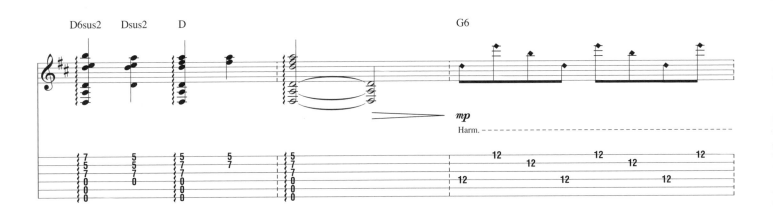

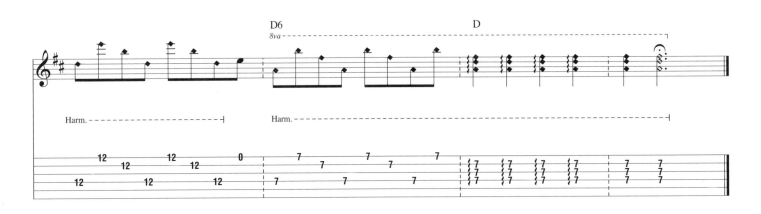

Avalon Blues
Words and Music by Mississippi John Hurt

A = 451 Hz

Intro
Moderately ♩ = 89

*Chord symbols reflect implied harmony.

1. Got to New York

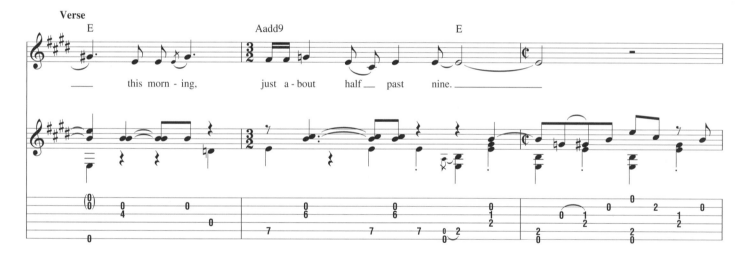

Verse

_____ this morn - ing,   just a - bout   half _ past   nine. _____

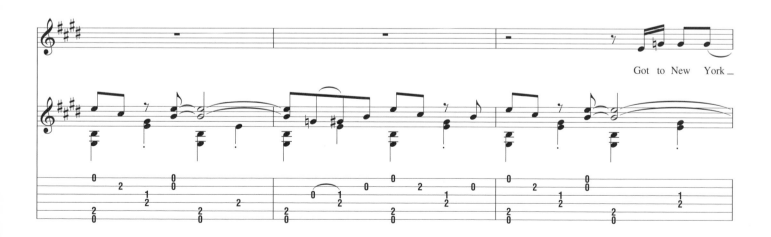

Got to New York _

this morn - in', just a - bout half past nine.

Hol - l'rin' one morn - in' in Av - 'lon, could - n't hard -

- ly keep from cry'n'.

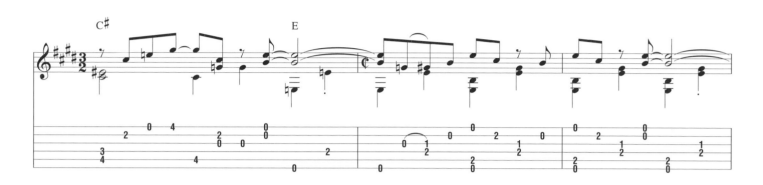

3. The train _____

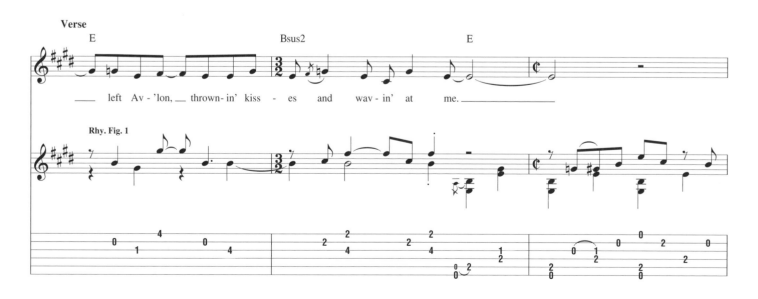

Verse

_____ left Av - 'lon, _____ thrown-in' kiss - es and wav - in' at me. _____

Rhy. Fig. 1

When the train ___

left Av-'lon, ___ thrown-in' kiss - es and ___ wav-in' at me. ___

Just come back, ___

___ dad-dy, and stay ___ right here ___ with me. ___

End Rhy. Fig. 2

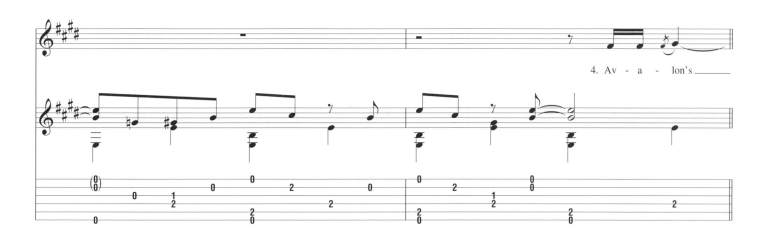

4. Av - a - lon's _____

Verse

Gtr. 1: w/ Rhy. Fig. 1

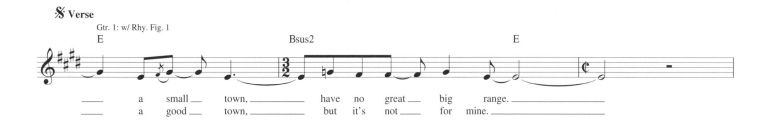

E   Bsus2   E

_____ a small _____ town, _____ have no great _____ big range. _____
_____ a good _____ town, _____ but it's not _____ for mine. _____

Av - a - lon's _____
New York's _____

Gtr. 1: w/ Rhy. Fig. 1 (last 4 meas.)

A/E   E

_____ a small _____ town, _____ have no great _____ big range. _____
_____ a good _____ town, _____ but it's not _____ for mine. _____

Pret - ty ma - mas
Go - in' back ___

To Coda ⊕

Gtr. 1: w/ Rhy. Fig. 2

B6(no 3rd)   C#   E

in Av - 'lon, ___ they sure ___ will spend ___ your change. ___
___ to Av-'lon, near where I have a pret - ty ma-ma all the time. ___

Guitar Solo

E   E/A   Eadd4   E

A   E

B6   C#   E

D.S. al Coda

5. New York's ___

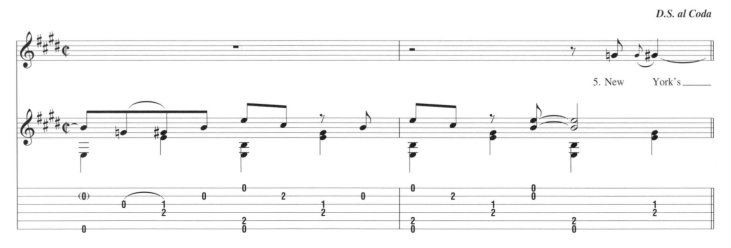

from Simon & Garfunkel - *Sounds of Silence*

Anji

Words and Music by Davy Graham

Gtr. 1: Capo II

5th & 6th strings only. *****Symbols in parentheses represent chord names respective to capoed guitar. Symbols above reflect actual sounding chords. Capoed fret is "0" in tab. Chord symbols reflect implied harmony.

***T = Thumb on 6th string

†Downstroke

*Slap strings w/ right hand fingers.

from The Beatles - (White Album)

Blackbird

Words and Music by John Lennon and Paul McCartney

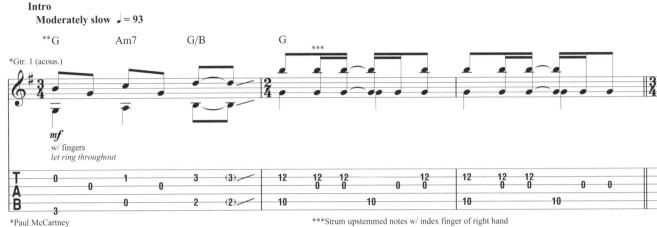

*Gtr. 1 (acous.)

mf
w/ fingers
let ring throughout

*Paul McCartney
**Chord symbols reflect implied harmony.

***Strum upstemmed notes w/ index finger of right hand
whenever more than one upstemmed note appears.

Verse

1., 2., 3. Black - bird sing - ing in the dead of night, ____

(1., 3.) take these bro - ken wings ____ and learn ____ to fly. ____
(2.) take these sunk - en eyes ____ and learn ____ to see. ____

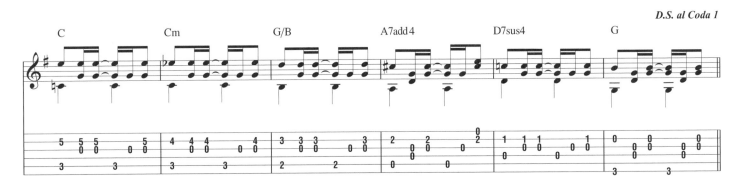

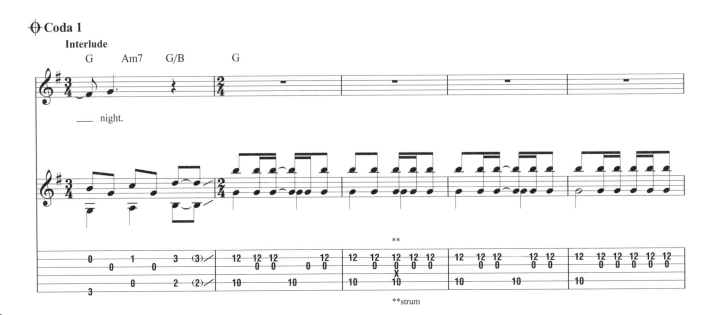

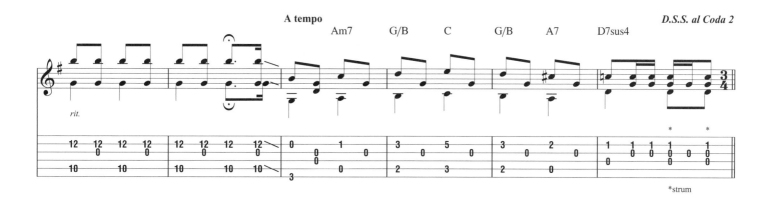

rit.

*strum

⊕ Coda 2

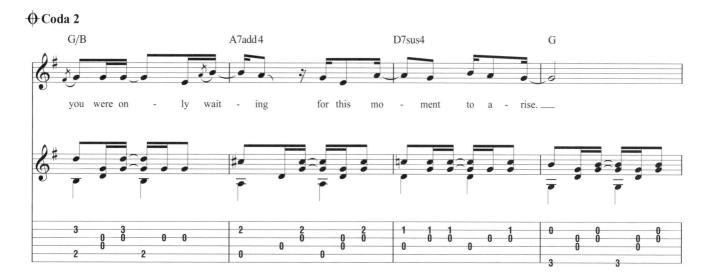

you were on - ly wait - ing for this mo - ment to a - rise.___

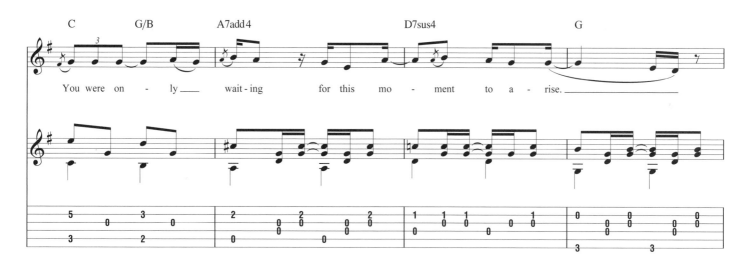

You were on - ly ___ wait - ing for this mo - ment to a - rise. ___

You were on - ly wait - ing ___ for this mo - ment to a - rise. ___

**Pat strings with fingers of right hand.

from Simon & Garfunkel - *Bridge Over Troubled Water*

The Boxer

Words and Music by Paul Simon

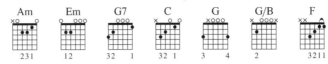

Gtr. 1: Tuning, Capo IV:
(low to high) E-A-D-G-B-D

Gtrs.2, 3 & 4: Tune down 1/2 step:
(low to high) E♭-A♭-D♭-G♭-B♭-E♭

Gtr. 5: Open C tuning, down 1/2 step:
(low to high) B-F♯-B-F♯-B-D♯

Intro
Moderately ♩ = 90

*Baby Martin arr. for gtr.

**Symbols in parentheses represent chord names respective to capoed guitar.
Symbols above reflect actual sounding chords. Capoed fret is "0" in tab.
Chord symbols reflect implied harmony.

Verse

34

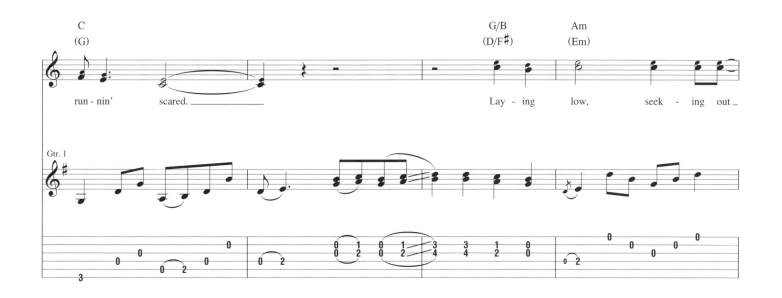

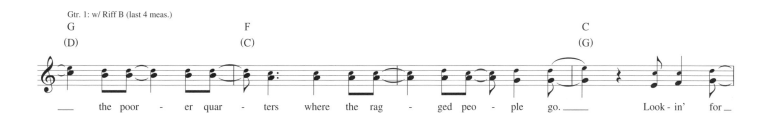

%Chorus

2nd time, Gtr. 4 tacet

when I was so lone-some, I took some com-fort there. La, la, la,

la, la, la, la.

Gtr. 2: w/ Riff C (1st meas., 3 times)

Gtr. 1

Gtr. 2: w/ Riff A

Guitar Solo

Gtr. 1: w/ Riff B
Gtr. 2: w/ Fill 2

Gtr. 2: w/ Riff B1 (last 14 meas.)

*Gtr. 4 (elec.)

**p < f
w/ clean tone

*Steel guitar arr. for gtr.

**Vol. swell

Rhy. Fig. 2

Gtr. 3

(cont. in slashes)

Fill 2

Gtr. 2

41

Gtr. 2: w/ Riff C

Gtr. 3

(cont. in notation)

Gtr. 1

Gtr. 5 (Dobro)

mf

w/ slide

Gtr. 1: w/ Riff D

5. In the clear-

Gtr. 5

Gtr. 3

Verse

Gtrs. 1 & 2: w/ Riffs B & B1 (1st 15 meas.)
Gtr. 3: w/ Rhy. Fig. 2
Gtr. 5 tacet

-ing stands a box-   er,   and a fight-   er   by his trade,   and he car-

-ries the re-mind-   ers   of ev-er-y glove __ that laid __ him down or

Outro
Gtrs. 1 & 2: w/ Riffs B & B1 (1st 15 meas.)
Gtr. 3: w/ Rhy. Fig. 2

from Chet Atkins - *Guitar Legend: The RCA Years*

Cascade

Written by Gene Slone

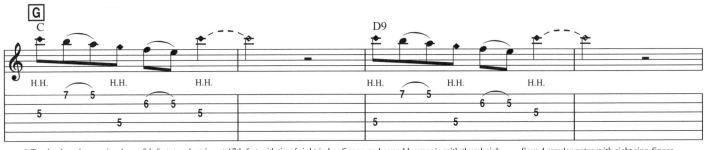

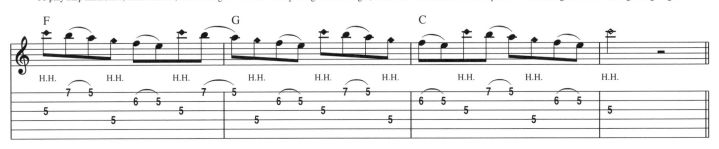

* To play harp harmonics, barre 5th fret, touch string at 17th fret with tip of right index-finger, and sound harmonic with thumbpick.   Sound regular notes with right ring-finger.

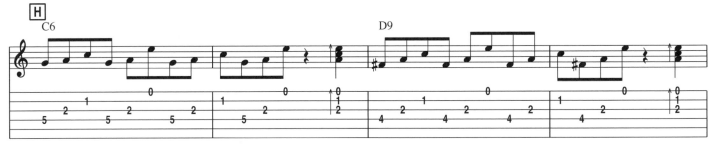

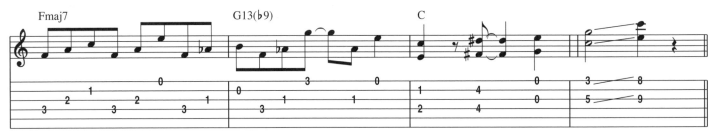

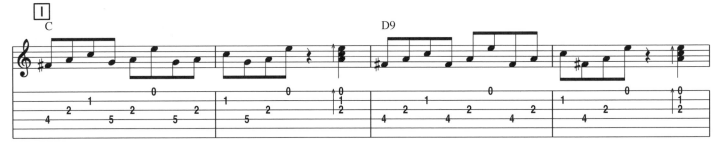

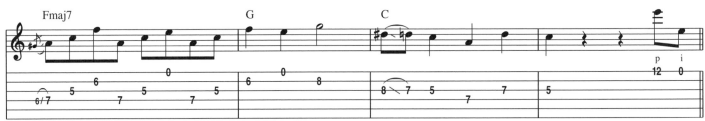

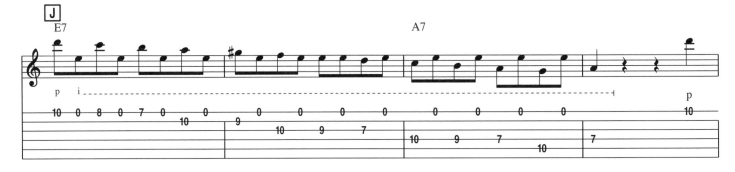

Causeway

Composed by Alex de Grassi

Tuning:
(low to high) E-B-E-F#-B-E

*Chord symbols reflect implied harmony.

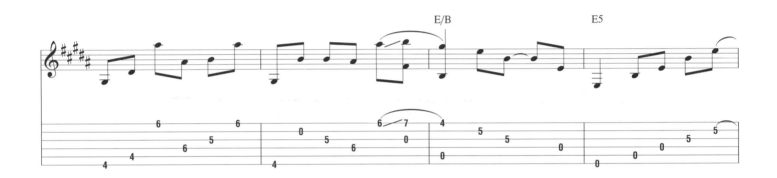

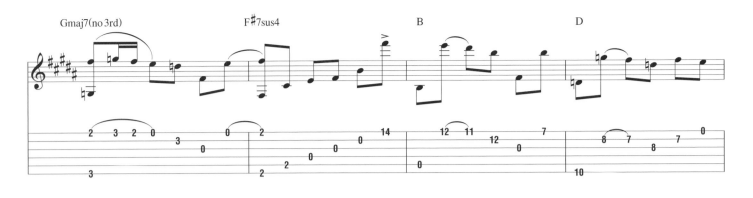

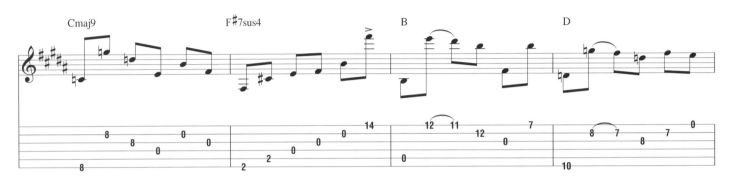

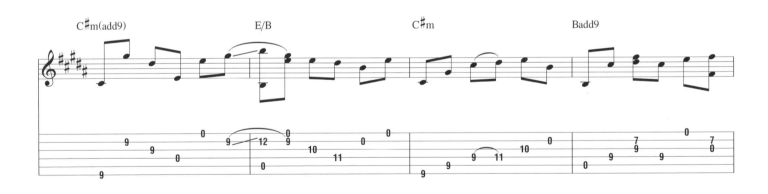

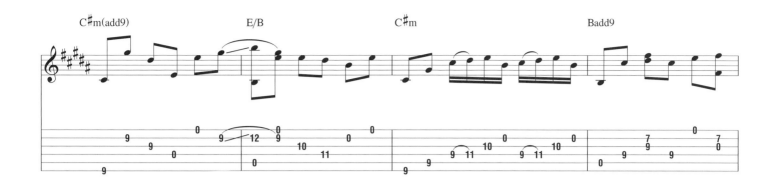

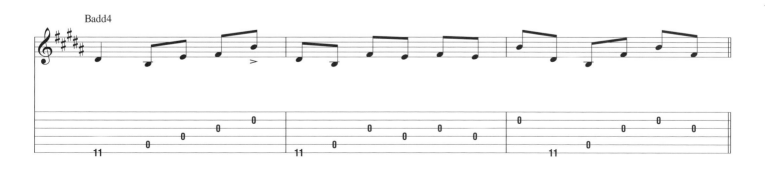

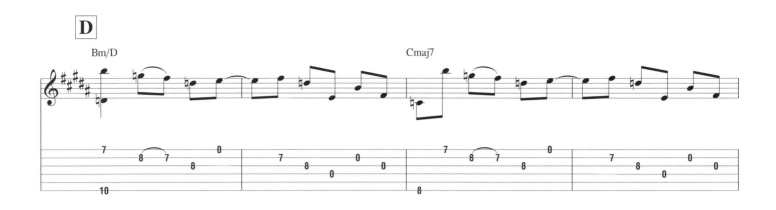

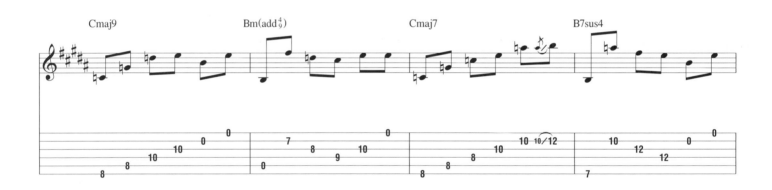

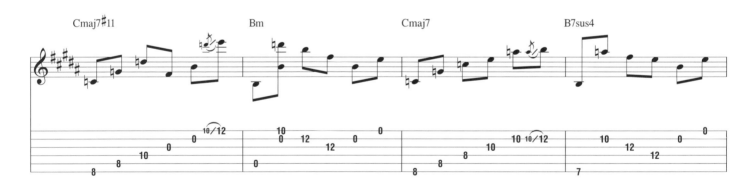

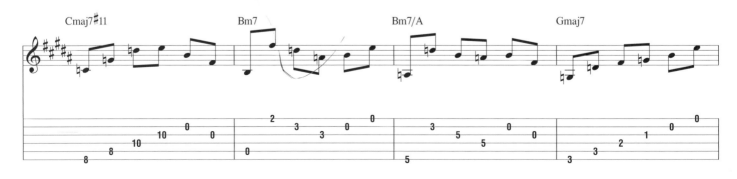

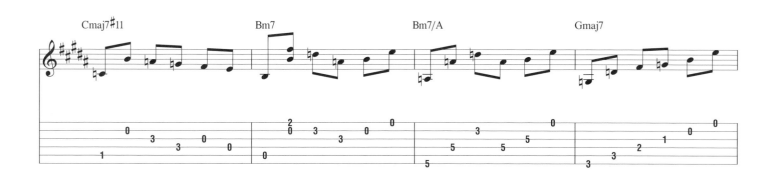

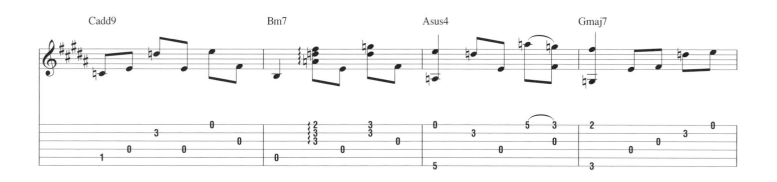

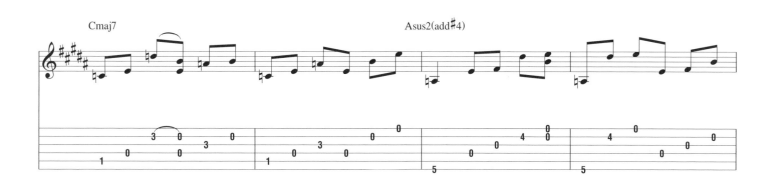

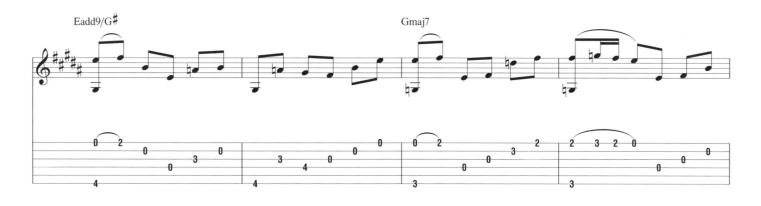

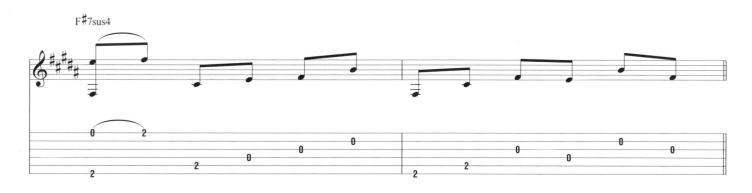

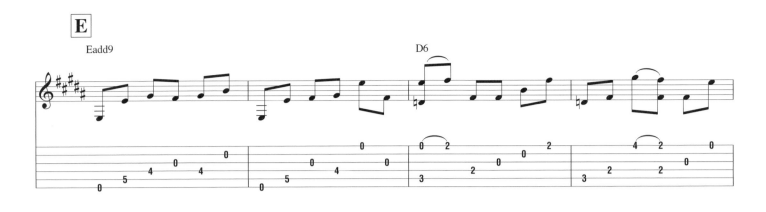

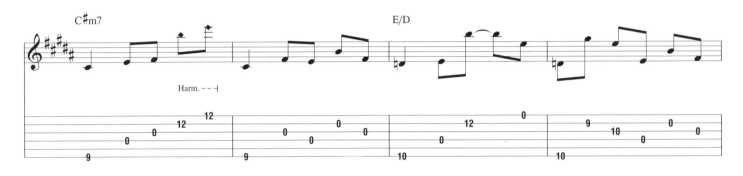

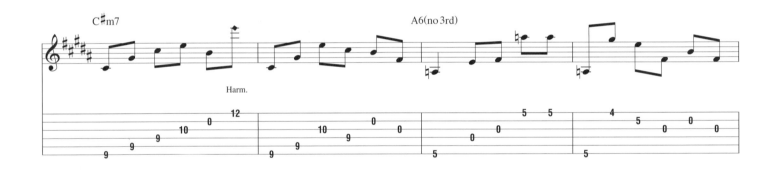

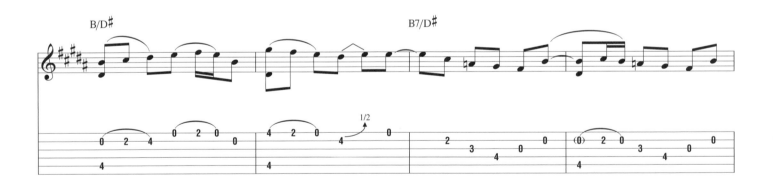

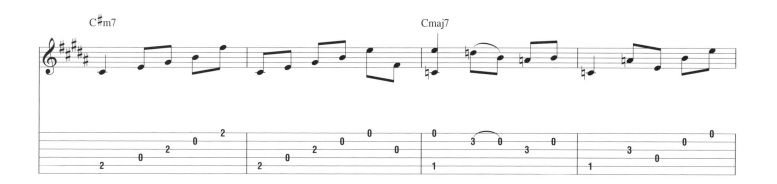

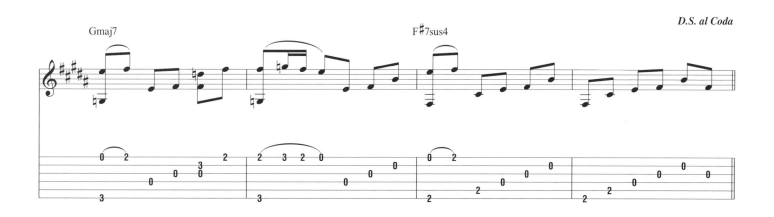

Coda

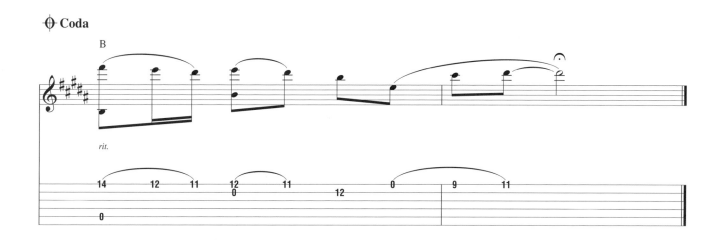

from *Original Motion Picture Soundtrack - THE DEER HUNTER*

Cavatina

from the Universal Pictures and EMI Films Presentation THE DEER HUNTER
By Stanley Myers

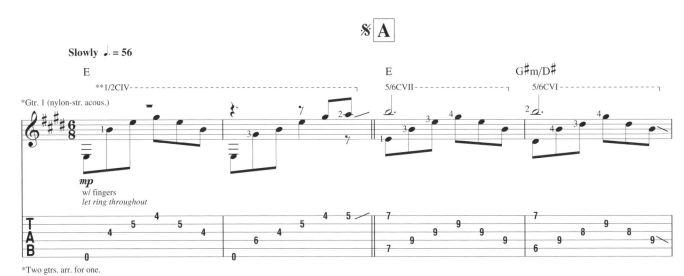

*Two gtrs. arr. for one.

****Traditional classical guitar barre indicated by "C." Fractional prefix denotes number of strings barred (1/2 = first 3 strings);
Roman numeral suffix indicates fret barred by index finger. Numbers on note staff indicate essential left hand fingerings for ease of playing.

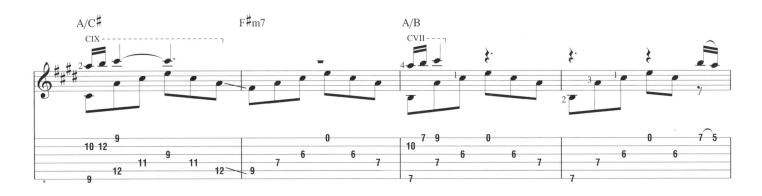

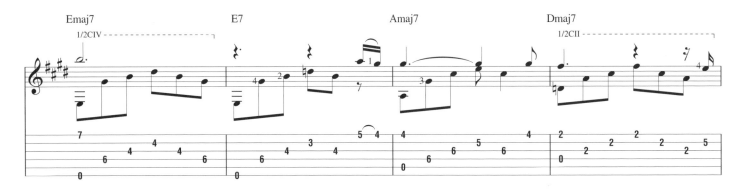

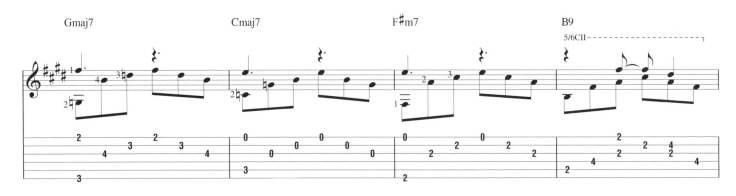

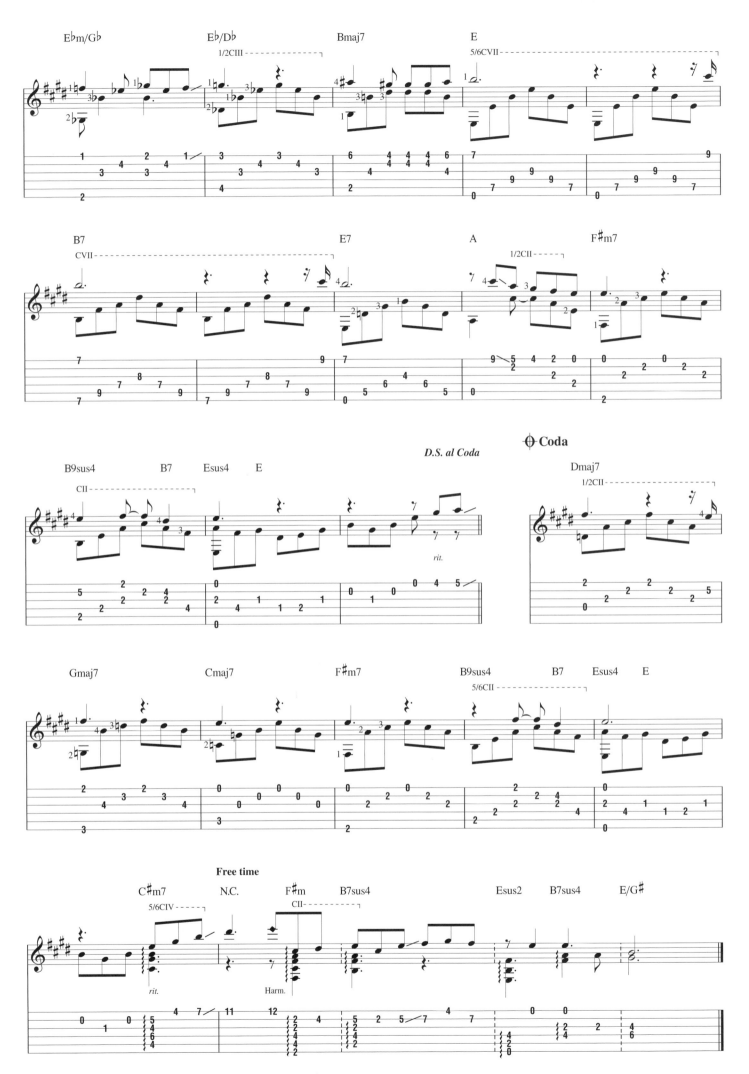

The Claw

By Jerry Reed

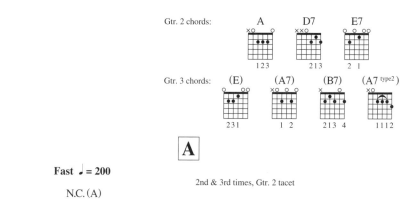

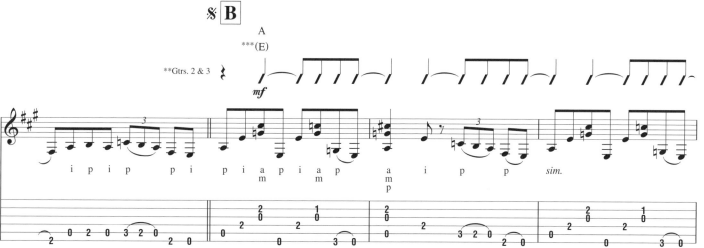

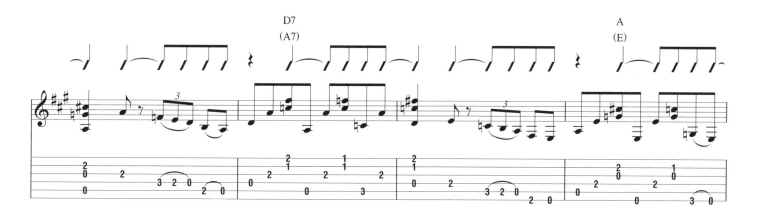

from Mason Williams - *Music 1968–1971*

Classical Gas

Music by Mason Williams

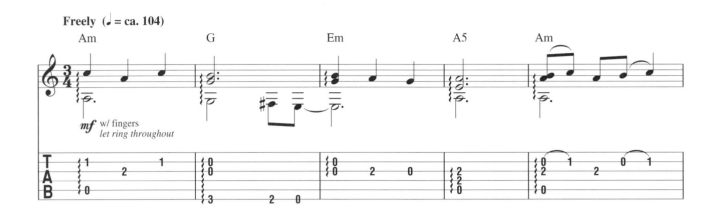

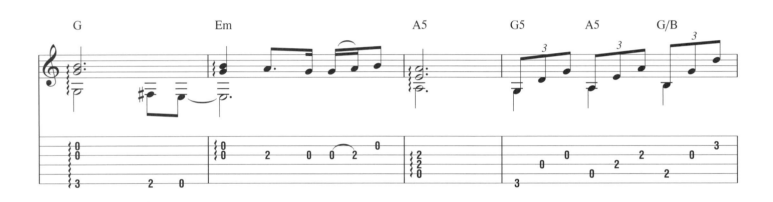

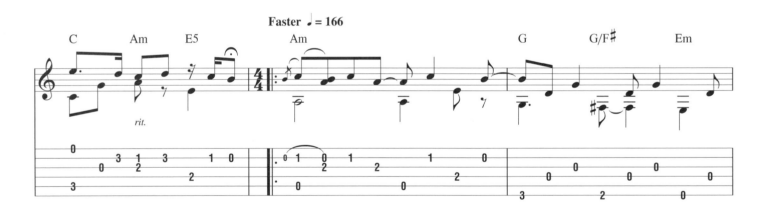

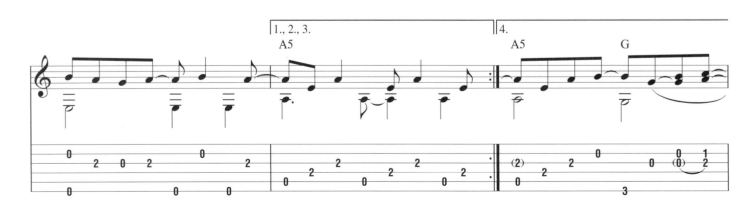

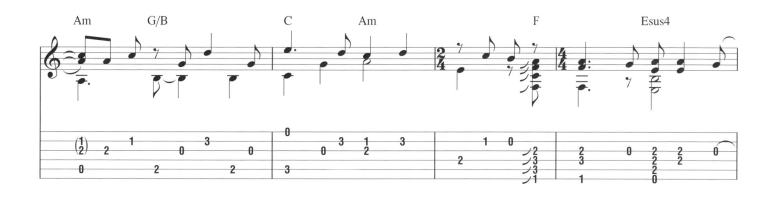

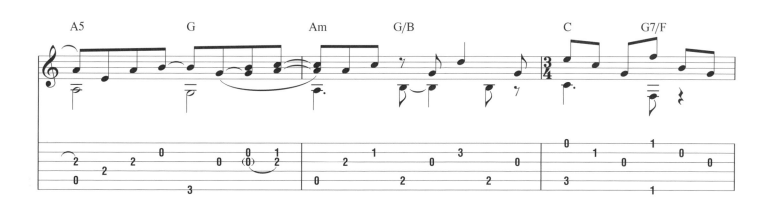

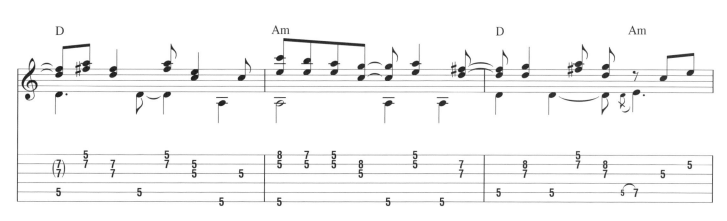

To Coda ⊕

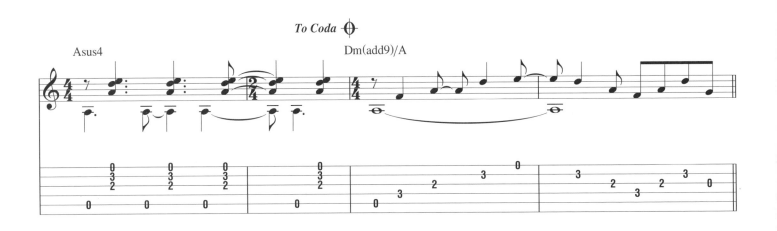

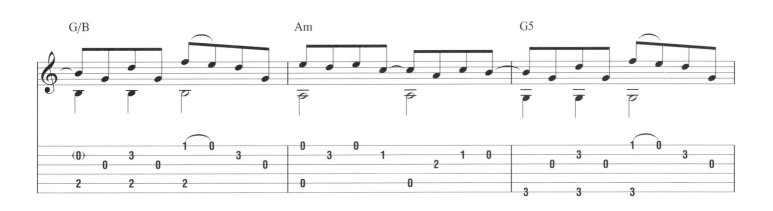

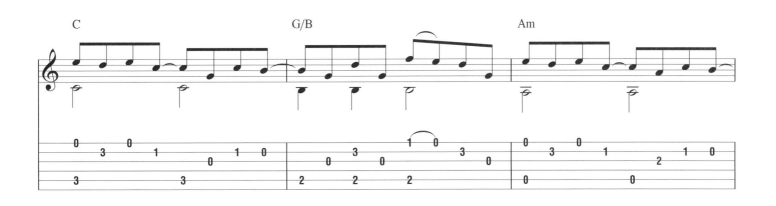

D.S. al Coda

 Coda

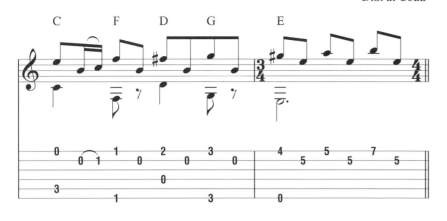

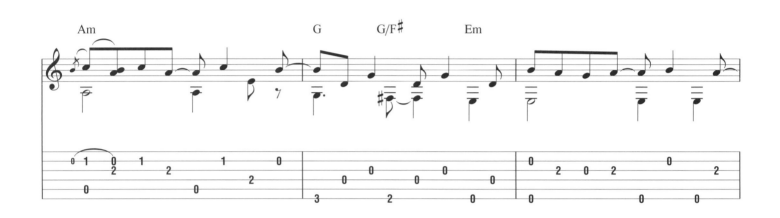

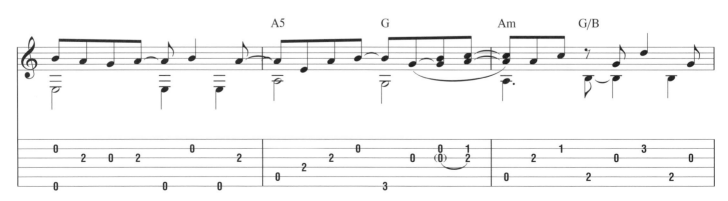

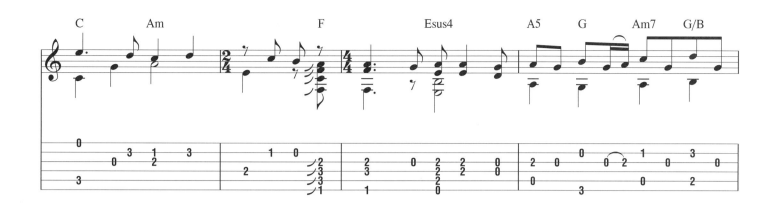

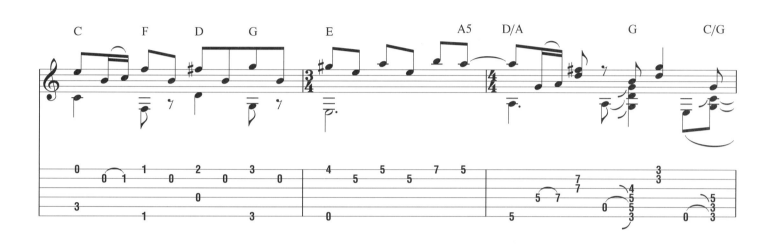

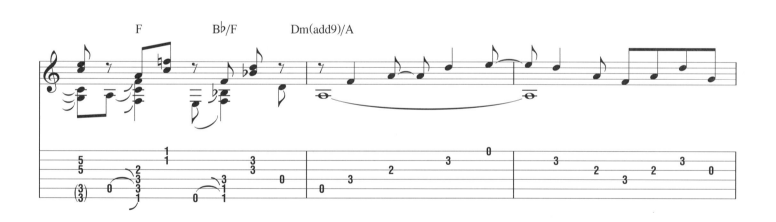

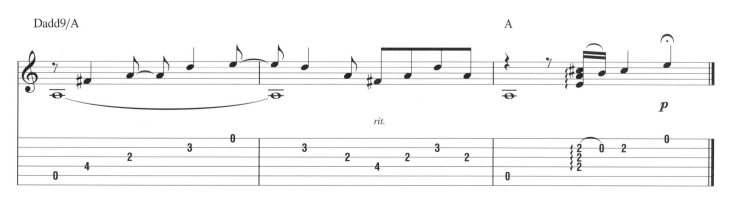

Cross Road Blues (Crossroads)

Words and Music by Robert Johnson

Open A Tuning, Down 1/2 Step; Capo II:

① = E♭ ④ = E♭
② = C   ⑤ = A♭
③ = A♭ ⑥ = E♭

Intro

Moderately ♩ = 95

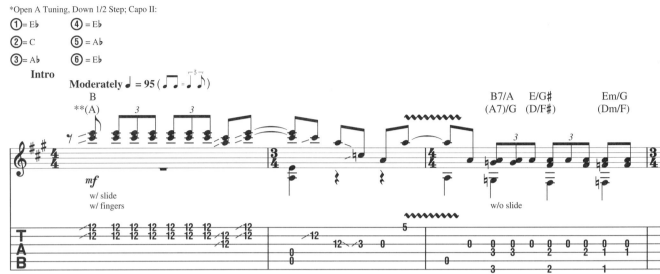

** Symbols in parentheses represent chord names (implied tonality) respective to capoed guitar.
Symbols above reflect harmony implied by vocals. Capoed fret is "0" in TAB.

Verse

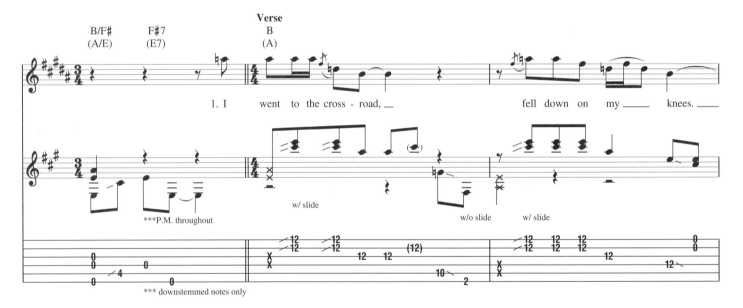

1. I went to the cross - road, ___ fell down on my ___ knees.

*** P.M. throughout

*** downstemmed notes only

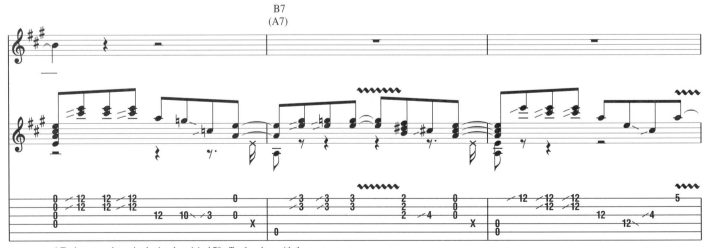

* Tunings were determined using the original 78s. To play along with the
Robert Johnson - The Complete Recordings CD set, Capo III.

run, _____ tell my friend-boy Wil-lie Brown. _____

Lord, that I'm

stand-in' at the cross-road, babe, I be-lieve I'm sink-in' down. _____

from Pierre Bensusan - *Près de Paris*

De Trilport A Fublaines

Traditional
Arranged by Pierre Bensusan

Tuning, Capo II:
(low to high) D-G-D-G-C-D

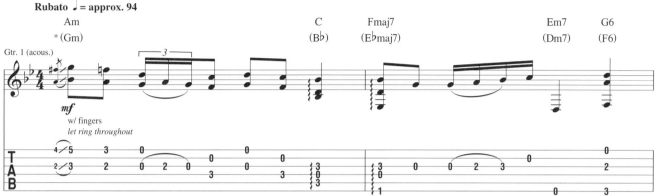

*Symbols in parentheses represent chord names respective to capoed guitar.
Symbols above reflect actual sounding chords. Capoed fret is "0" in tab.
Chord symbols reflect implied harmony.

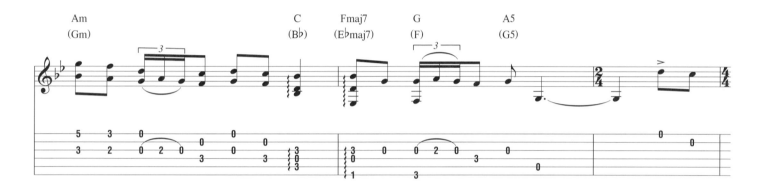

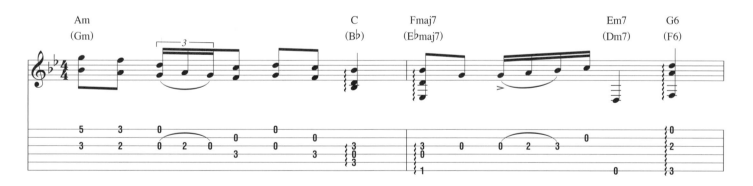

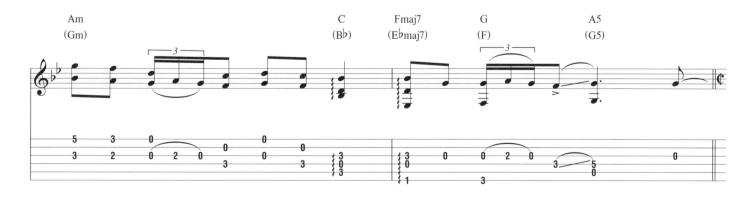

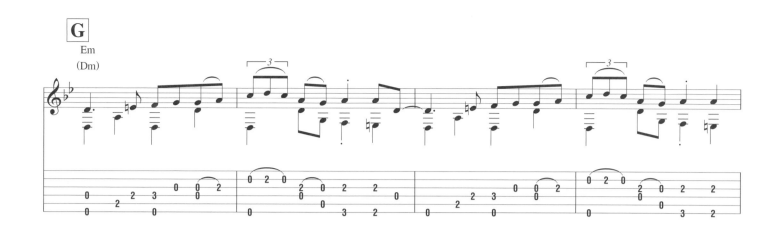

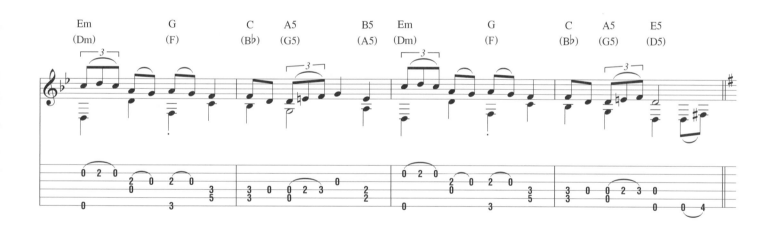

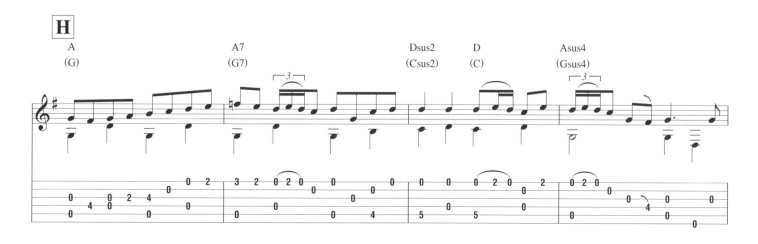

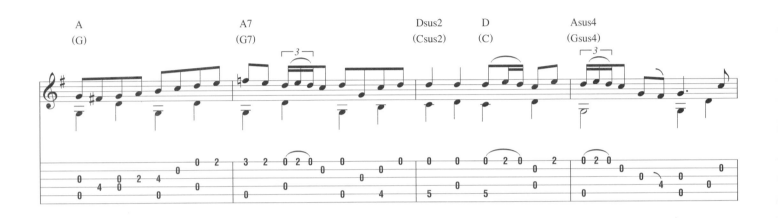

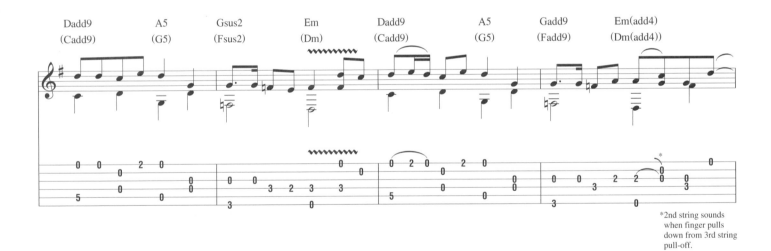

*2nd string sounds
when finger pulls
down from 3rd string
pull-off.

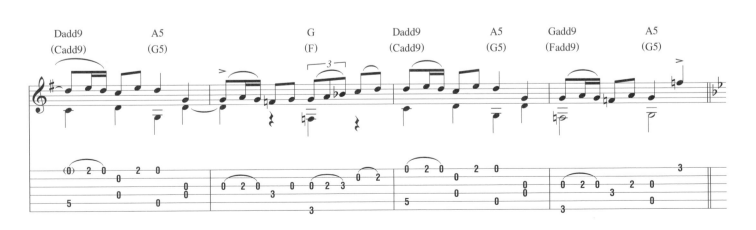

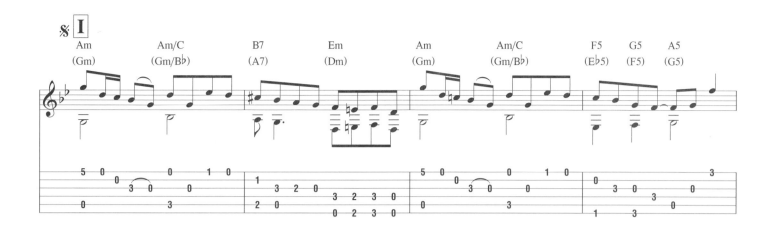

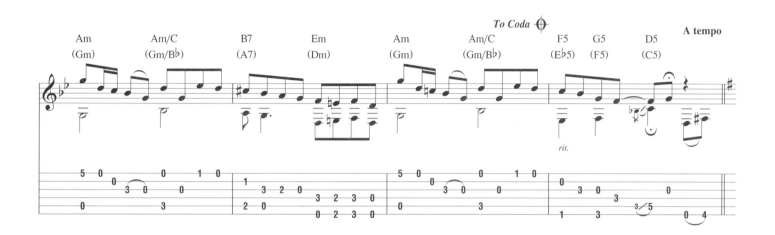

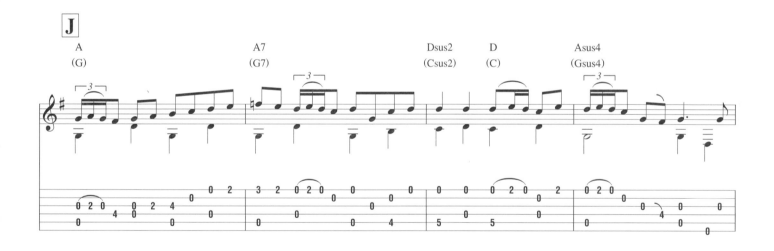

Deep River Blues

Traditional
Arranged and Adapted by Doc Watson

Tune up 1/2 step:
(low to high) F-B♭-E♭-A♭-C-F

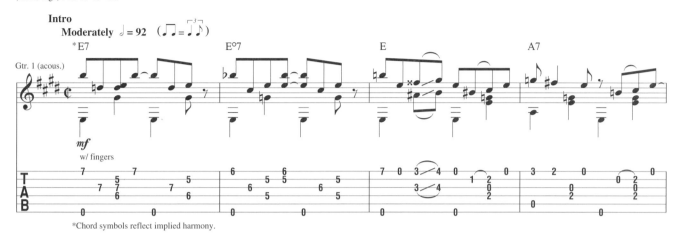

*Chord symbols reflect implied harmony.

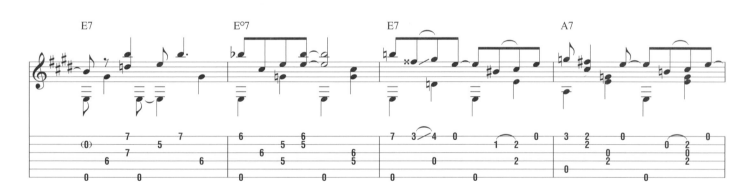

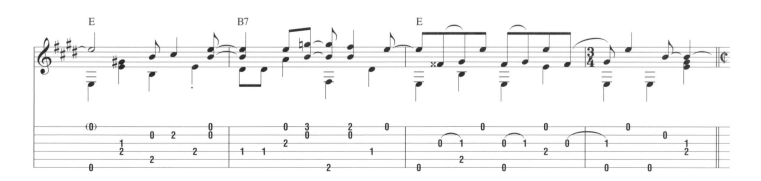

(4., 6.) let it rain, ___ let it pour, ___ let it rain ___ a whole lot more ___ 'cause I ___

___ got ___ them deep riv - er blues. ___

Let the rain ___ drive right on, ___ let ___ the waves ___ sweep a - long ___ 'cause I ___

To Coda ⊕

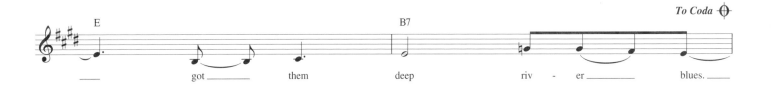

___ got ___ them deep riv - er ___ blues. ___

Guitar Solo

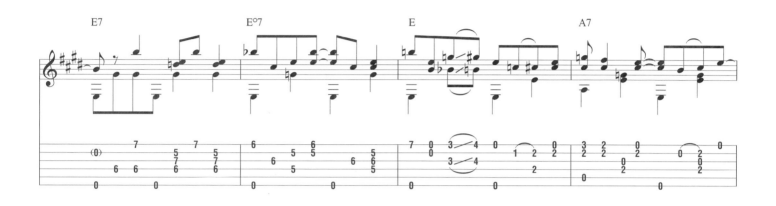

5. If _____

Verse

Gtr. 1: w/ Rhy. Fig. 1 (1st 12 meas.)

my boat sinks with me, I'll go down. Don't you see? 'Cause I

got them deep riv - er blues.

Now I'm gon - na say good - bye and if I sink, just let me die 'cause I

D.S. al Coda

got them deep riv - er blues.

Coda

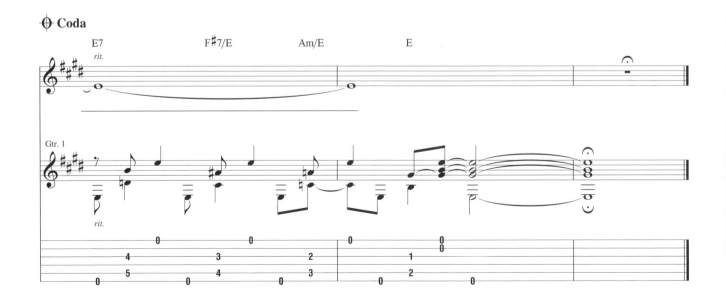

Desperate Man Blues

Written by John Fahey

Open G tuning:, down 1/2 step:
(low to high) D♭-G♭-D♭-G♭-B♭-D♭

A

Moderately ♩ = 98

*C/G

Gtr. 1 (acous.)

mf
w/ fingers

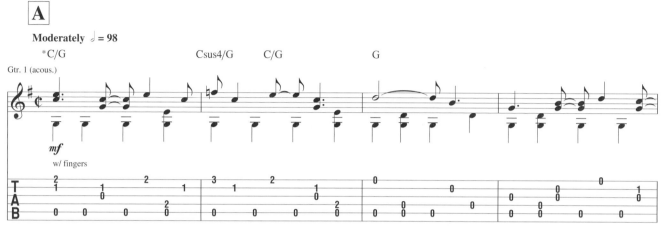

*Chord symbols reflect implied harmony.

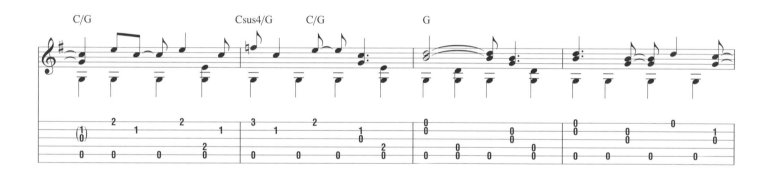

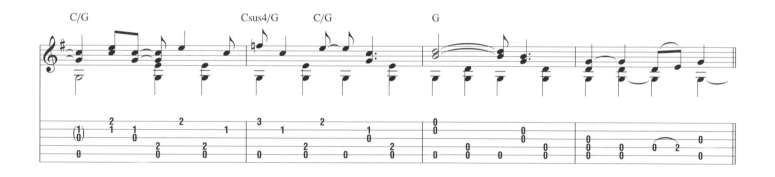

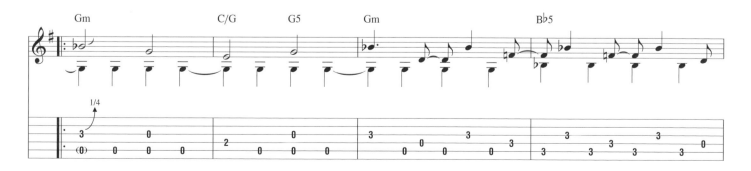

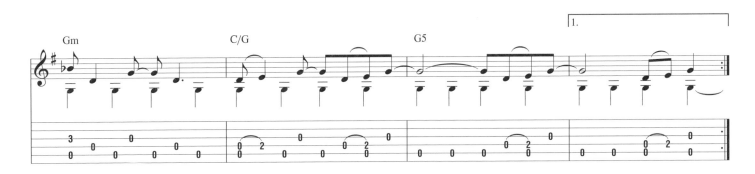

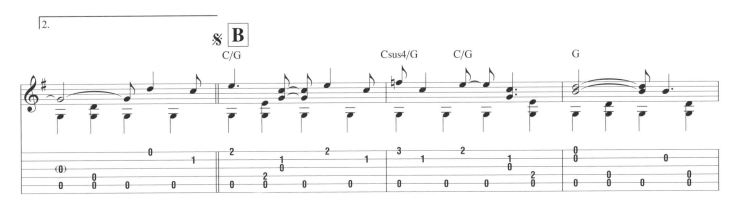

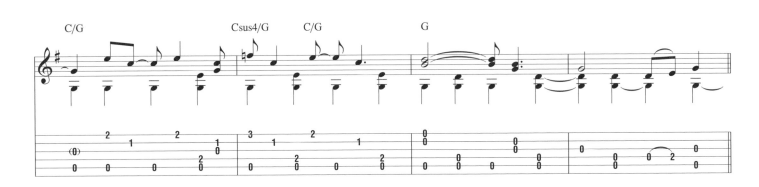

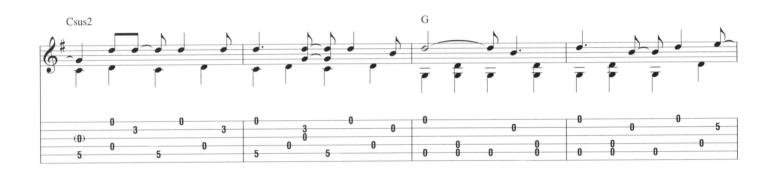

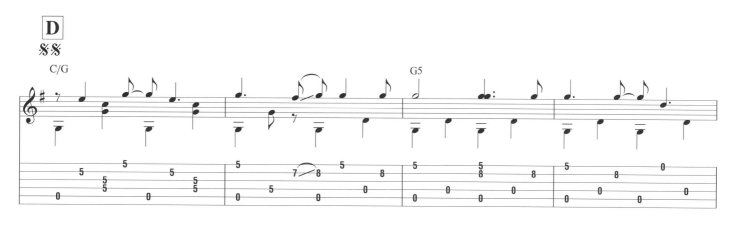

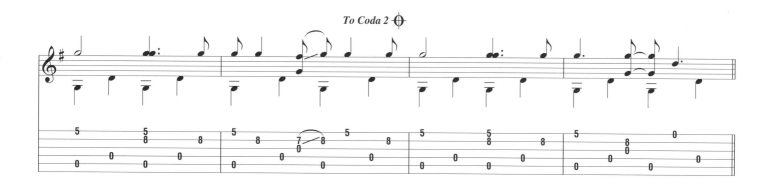

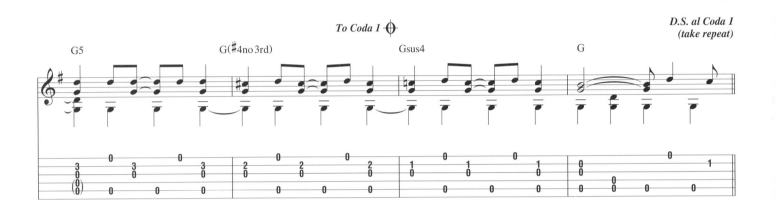

Coda 1

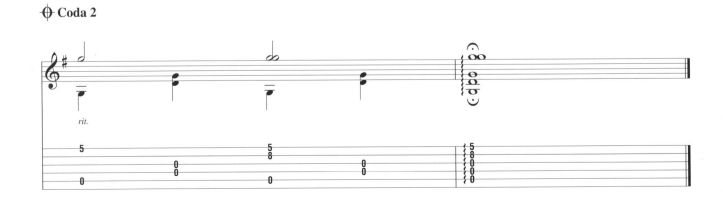

Coda 2

from Andy McKee - *Art of Motion*

Drifting

By Andy McKee

DADGAD tuning:
(low to high) D-A-D-G-A-D

Moderately ♩ = 125

E5

Gtr. 1 (acous.)

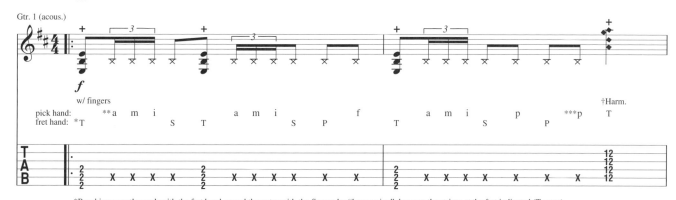

f

w/ fingers

pick hand: **a m i   a m i   f   a m i p   ***p
fret hand: *T   S T   S P   T   S   P   T

*Reaching over the neck with the fret hand, sound the notes with the fingers by "hammering" down on the strings at the fret indicated (T = tap).
S = slap face of gtr. at upper bout. P = slap palm on upper bout.

**Pick hand finger indications: a = ring, m = middle, i = index, f = all (executed on lower bout unless specified),
p = thumb tap on face of gtr. at lower bout. T = tap as above.

***Pick hand thumb at upper bout.

†Harmonics executed by slapping strings w/ pick hand index or middle finger.

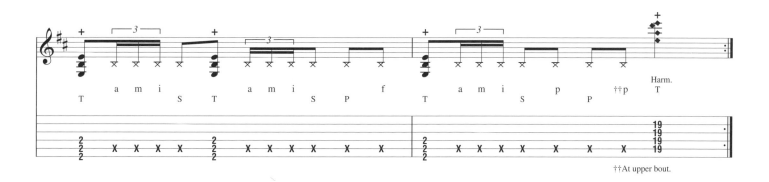

††At upper bout.

𝄋 **B**

Em9   G5   A

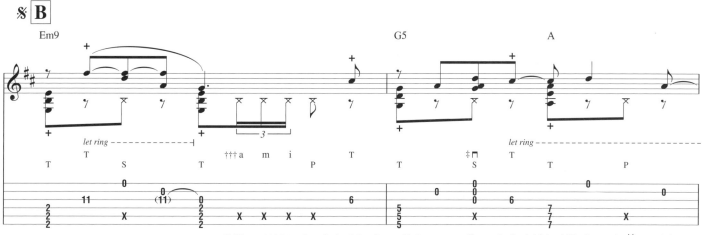

let ring   *let ring*

†††Tap next triplet on face of guitar below the sound hole.   ‡Strum w/ nails of pick hand (⊓ = downstroke, ⋁ = upstroke).

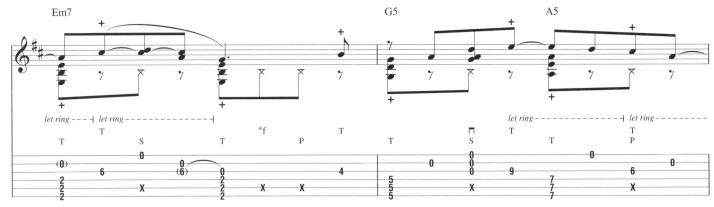

*Tap fingers on face of gtr. below sound hole.

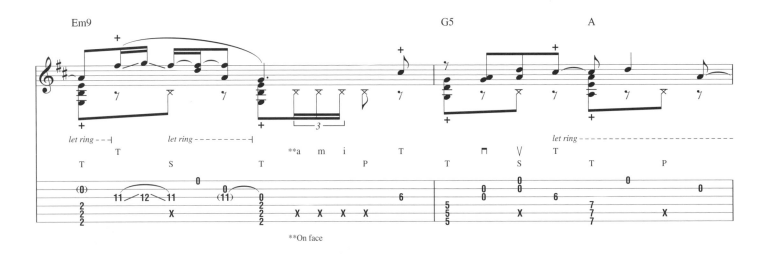

**On face

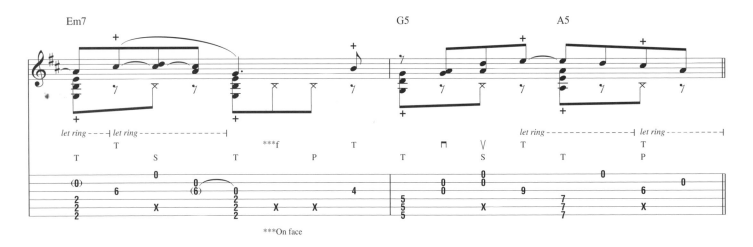

***On face

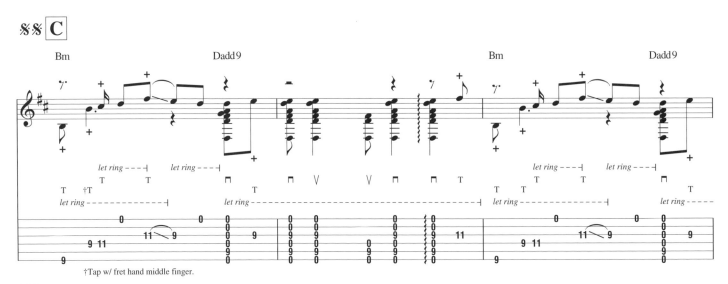

†Tap w/ fret hand middle finger.

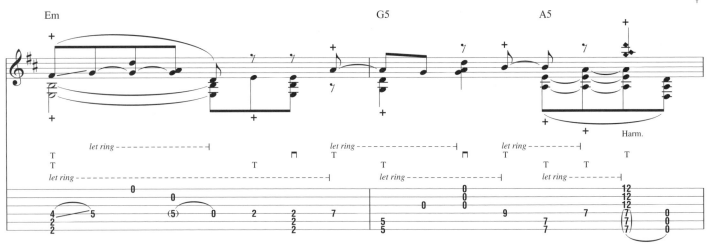

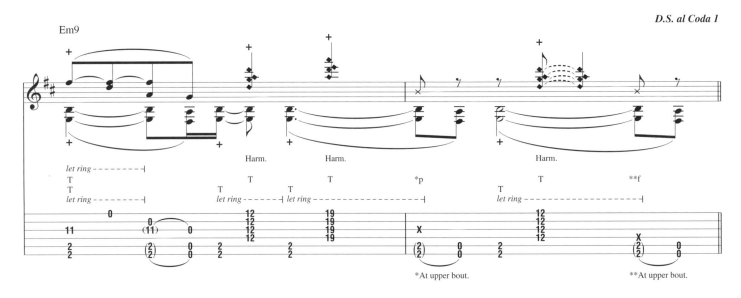

*At upper bout.   **At upper bout.

Coda 1

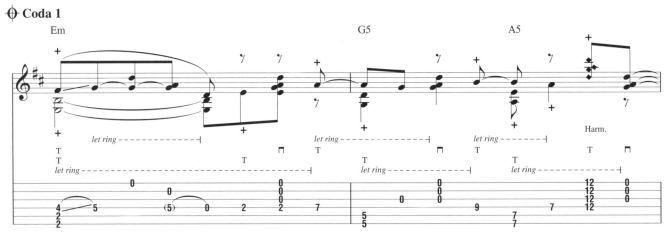

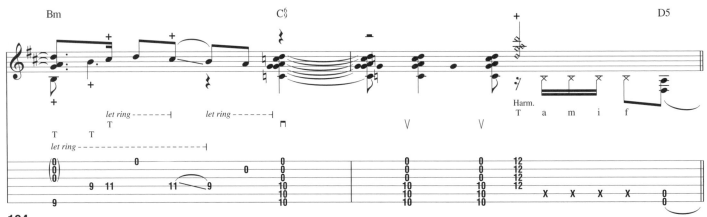

*Reach under neck w/ fret hand, next 8 meas.   **Thumb strum

***Thumb strum

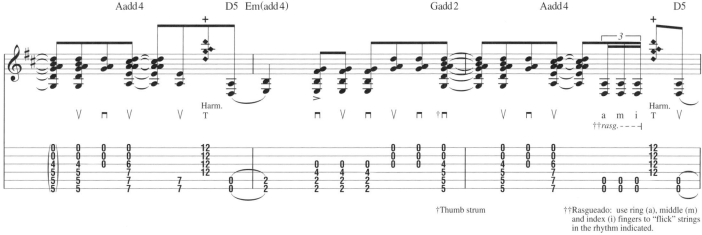

†Thumb strum

††Rasgueado: use ring (a), middle (m) and index (i) fingers to "flick" strings in the rhythm indicated.

D.S.S. al Coda 2

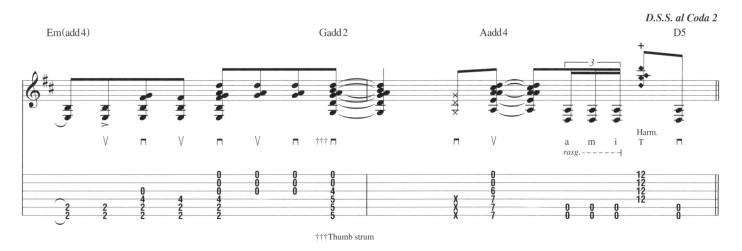

†††Thumb strum

⊕ Coda 2

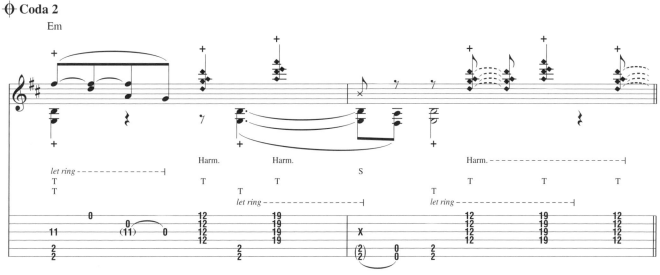

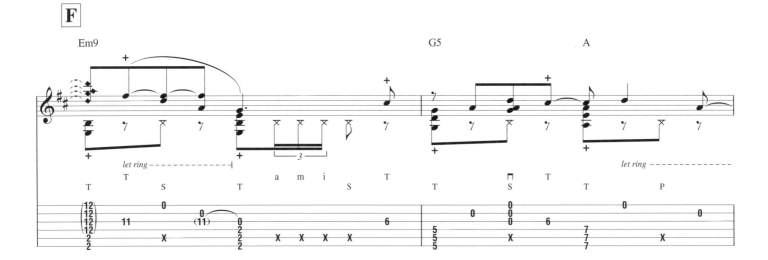

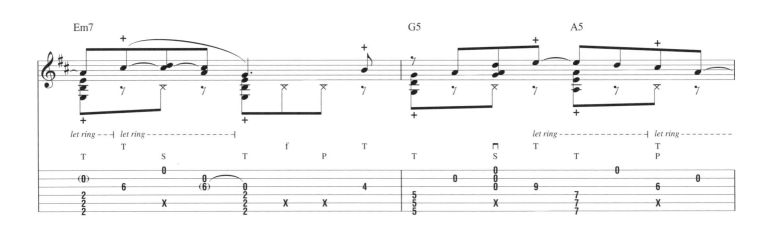

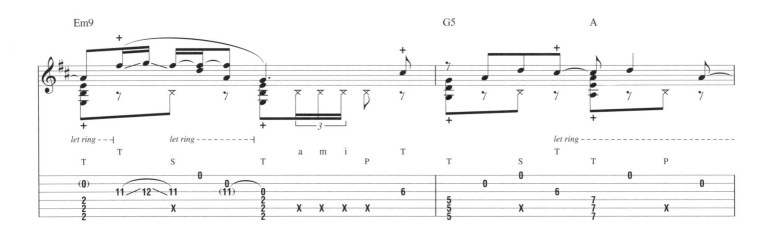

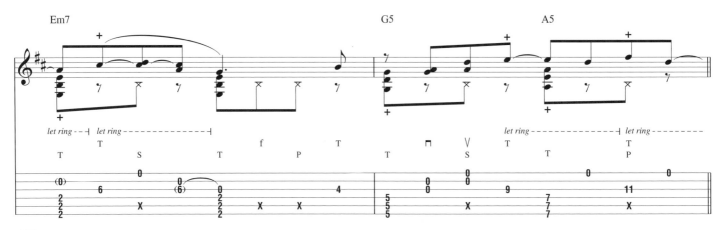

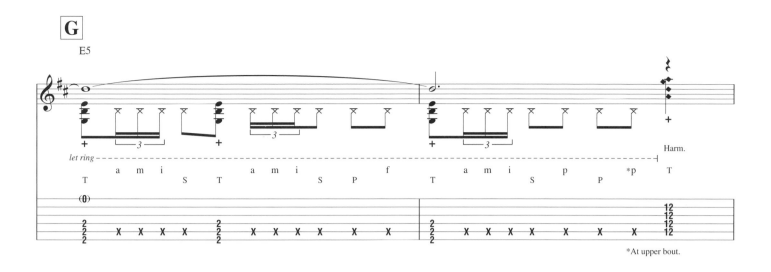

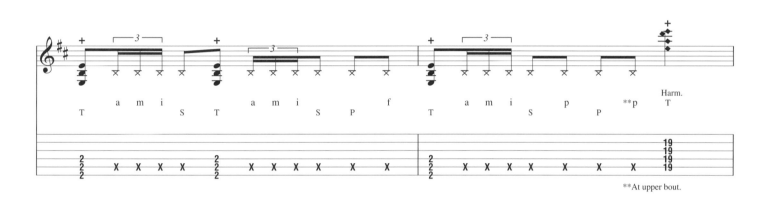

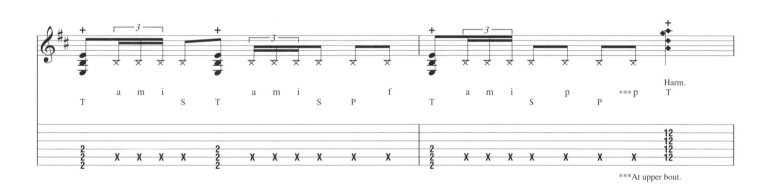

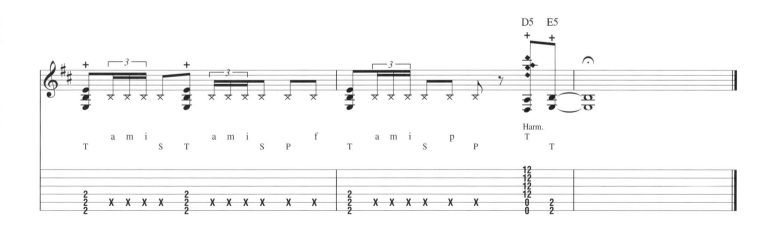

Dee

Music by Randy Rhoads

Slowly ♩ = 45

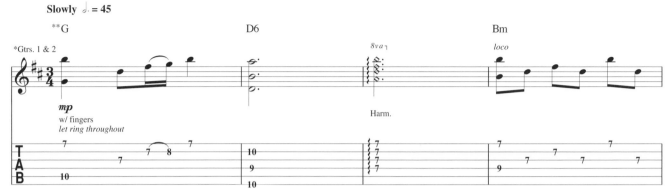

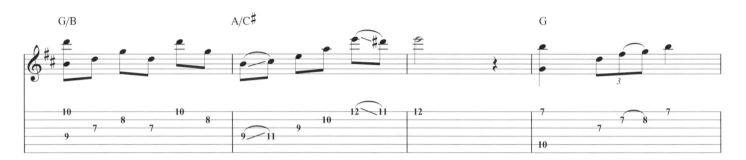

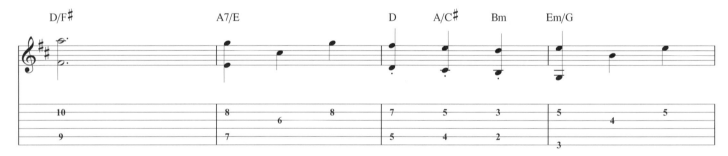

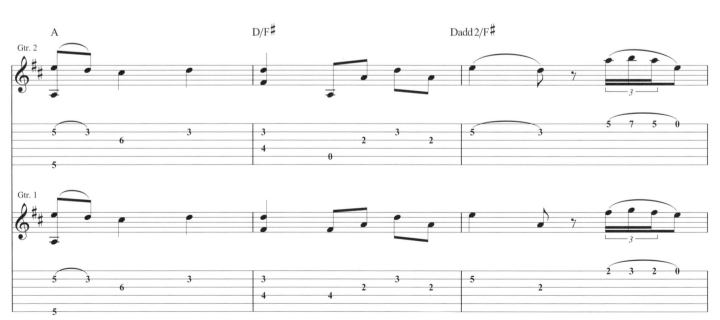

*Gtr. 2 to left of slashes in tab.

Dust in the Wind

Words and Music by Kerry Livgren

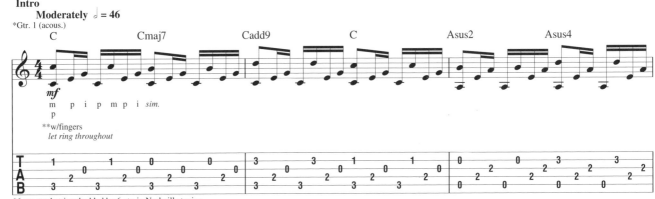

Intro
Moderately ♩ = 46
*Gtr. 1 (acous.)

*6-str. steel-string doubled by 6-str. in Nashville tuning.
**p=thumb, i=index, m=middle

Verse

1. I close my eyes, on - ly for a mo - ment, and the mo - ment's gone.
2. Same old song, just a drop of wa - ter in an end - less sea.
3. Now don't hang on, noth - ing lasts for - ev - er but the earth and sky.

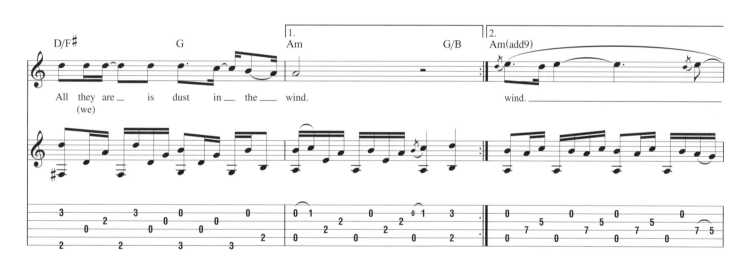

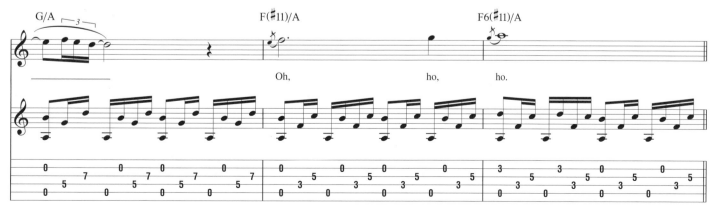

Instrumental Bridge

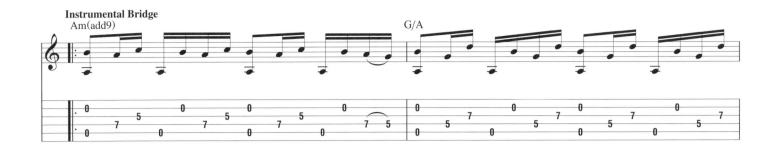

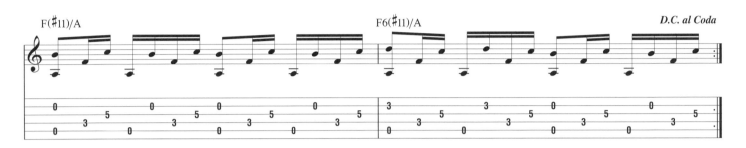

Coda

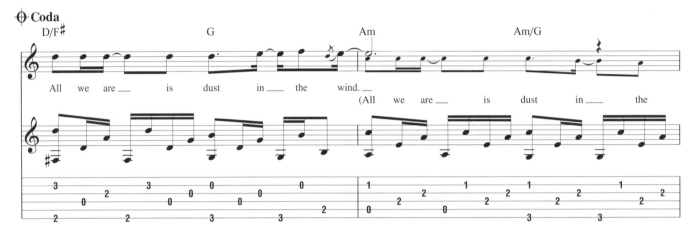

All we are ___ is dust in ___ the wind. ___

(All we are ___ is dust in ___ the

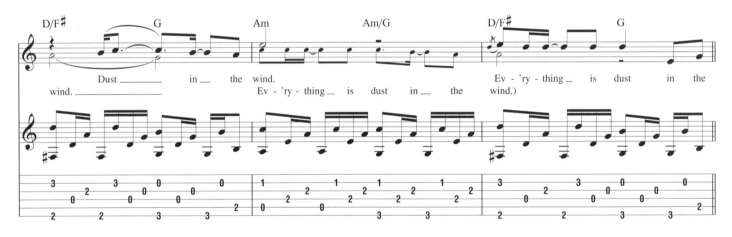

Dust ___ in ___ the wind.

wind. ___

Ev - 'ry - thing ___ is dust in ___ the wind.)

Ev - 'ry - thing ___ is dust in the

Outro

Play 4 Times and Fade

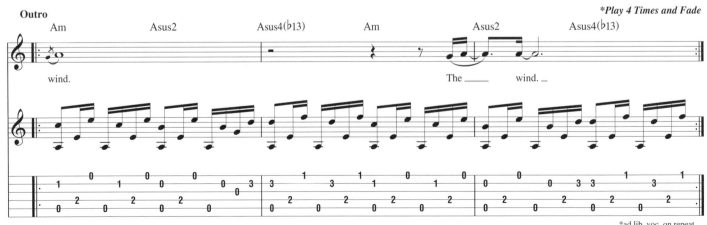

wind.

The ___ wind. ___

ad lib. voc. on repeat

Hard Time Killing Floor Blues

Words and Music by Nehemiah "Skip" James

Open Dm tuning:
(low to high) D-A-D-F-A-D

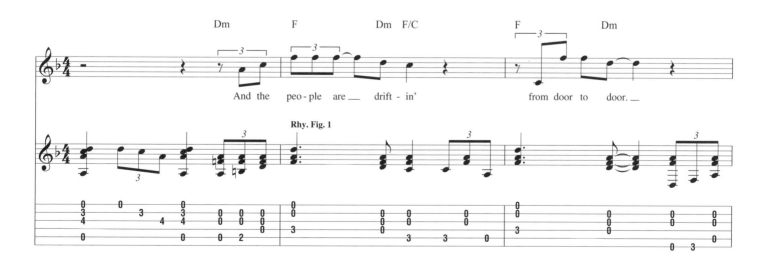

from *Crosby, Stills & Nash*

Helplessly Hoping

Words and Music by Stephen Stills

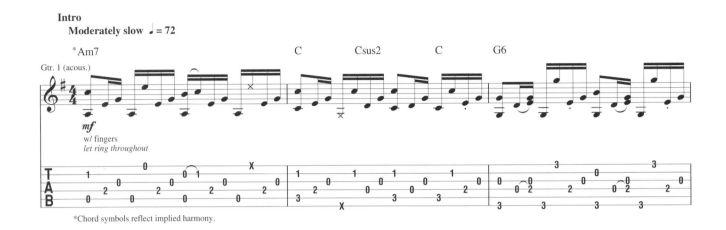

*Chord symbols reflect implied harmony.

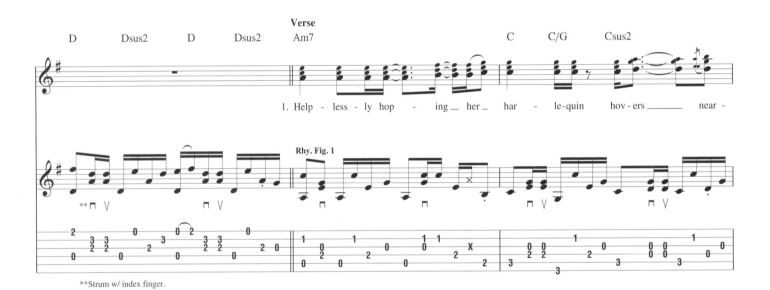

**Strum w/ index finger.

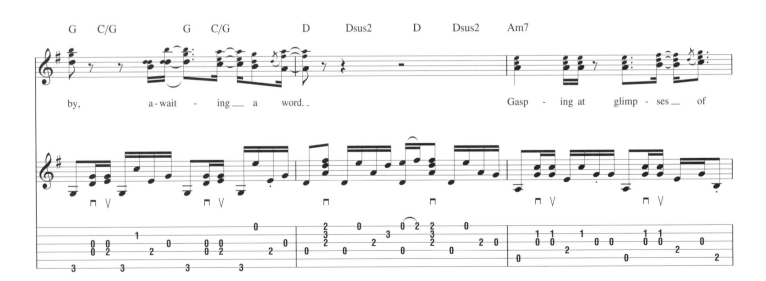

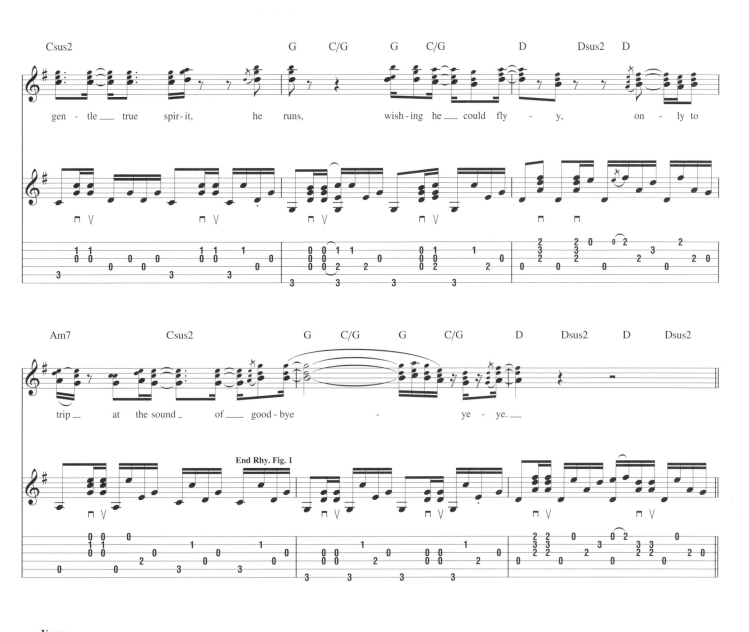

gen - tle ___ true spir-it, he runs, wish-ing he ___ could fly ___ -y, on - ly to

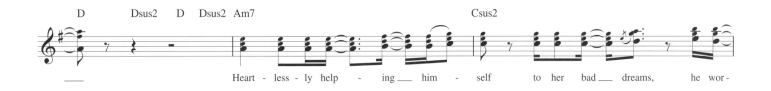

trip ___ at the sound ___ of ___ good - bye - ye - ye. ___

End Rhy. Fig. 1

Verse
Gtr. 1: w/ Rhy. Fig. 1

2. Word - less - ly watch - ing, ___ he ___ waits by the win - dow ___ and won - ders at the emp - ty place ___ in - side. ___

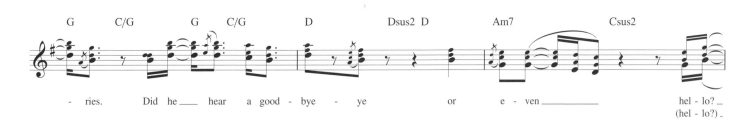

___ Heart - less - ly help - ing ___ him - self to her bad ___ dreams, he wor -

- ries. Did he ___ hear a good - bye - ye or e - ven ___ hel - lo?
(hel - lo?)

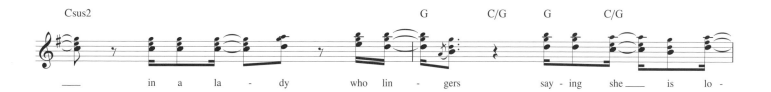

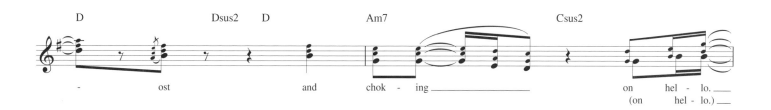

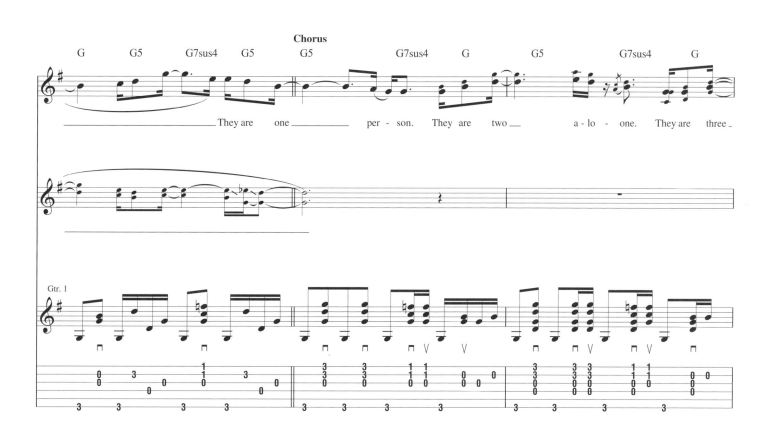

Jack Fig

By J.S. Bach
Arranged by Leo Kottke

Open G tuning, down 2 steps:
(low to high) B♭-E♭-B♭-E♭-G-B♭

Fast ♩ = 116

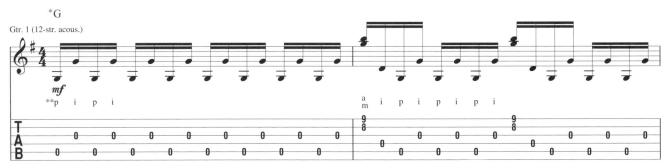

*Chord symbols reflect implied harmony.
**p = thumb, i = index, m = middle, a = ring

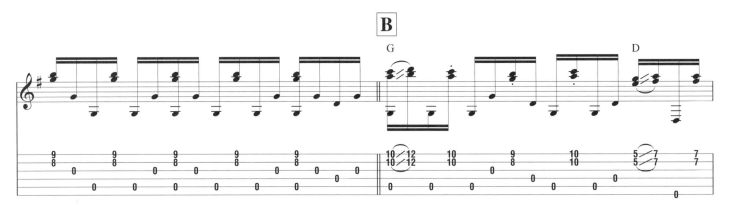

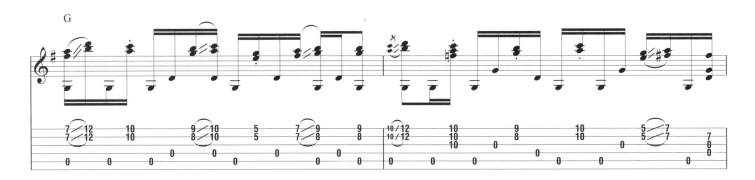

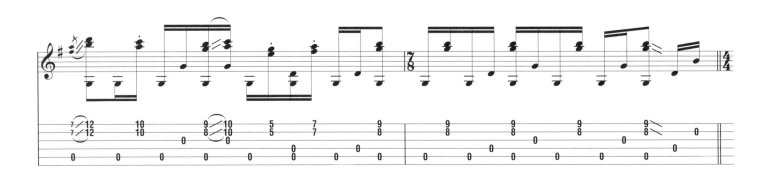

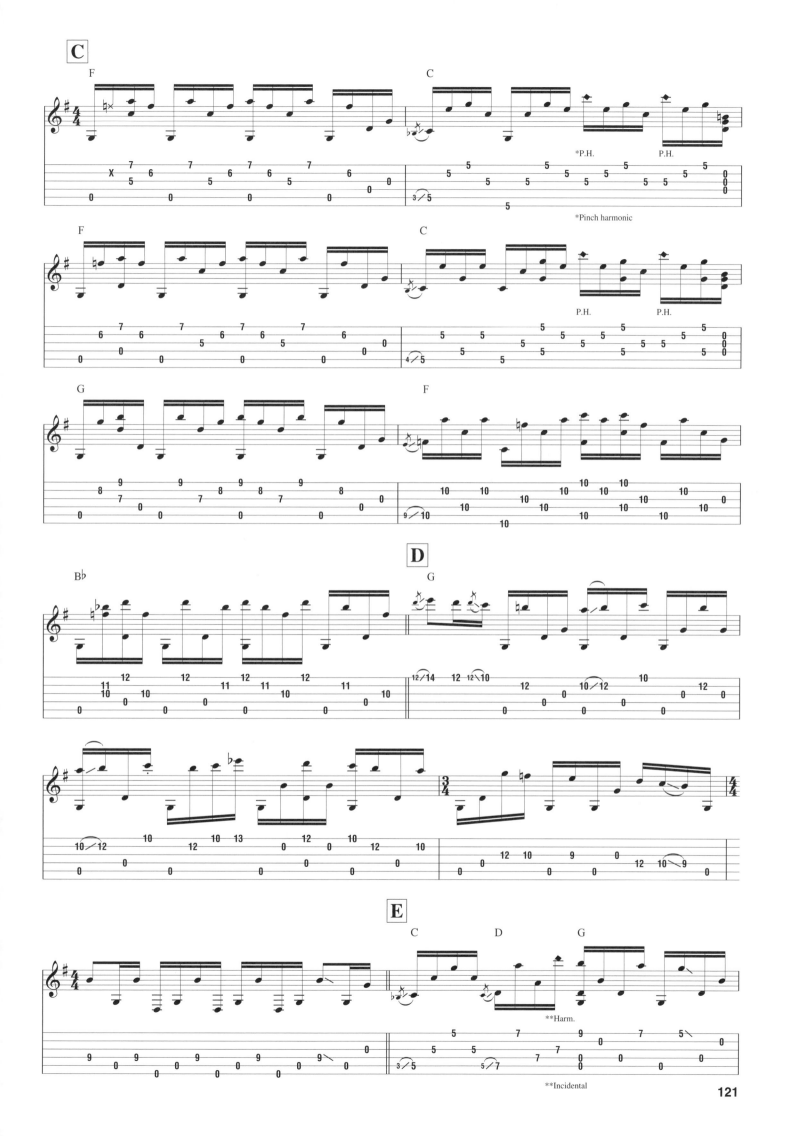

*Pinch harmonic

**Harm.

**Incidental

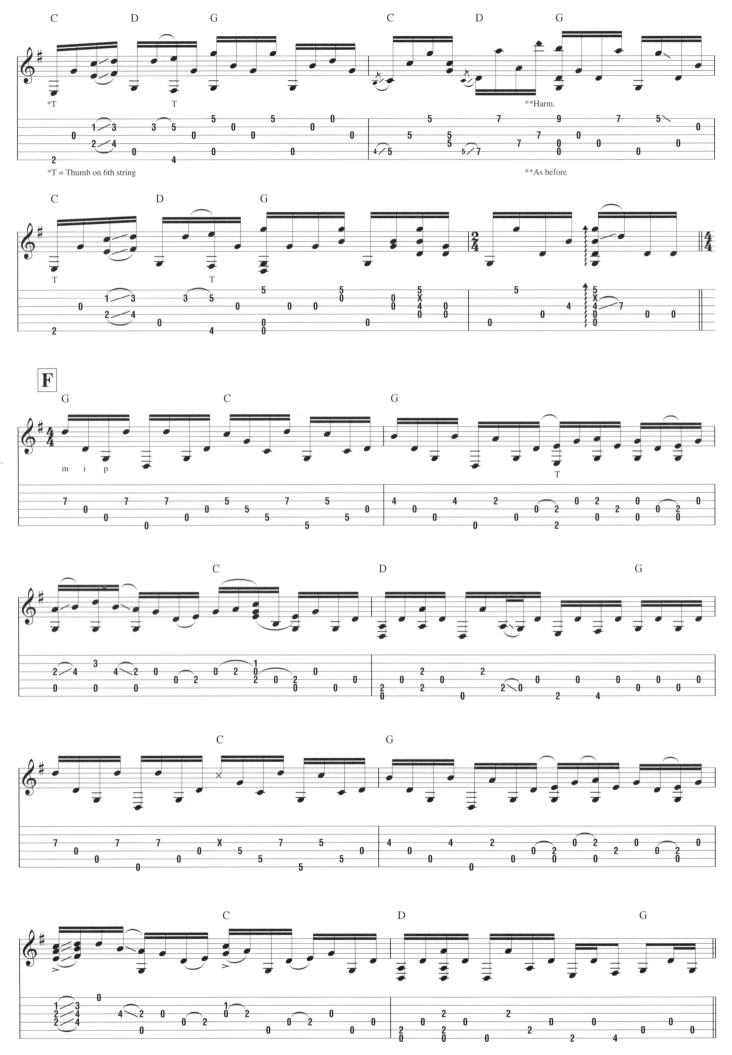

*T = Thumb on 6th string

**As before

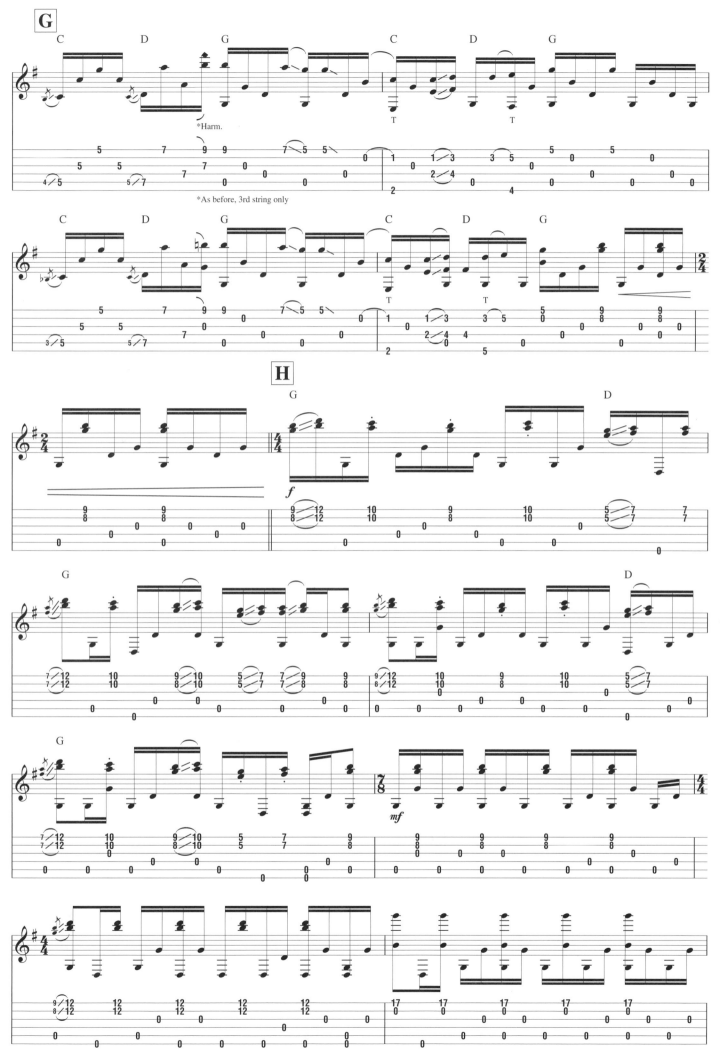

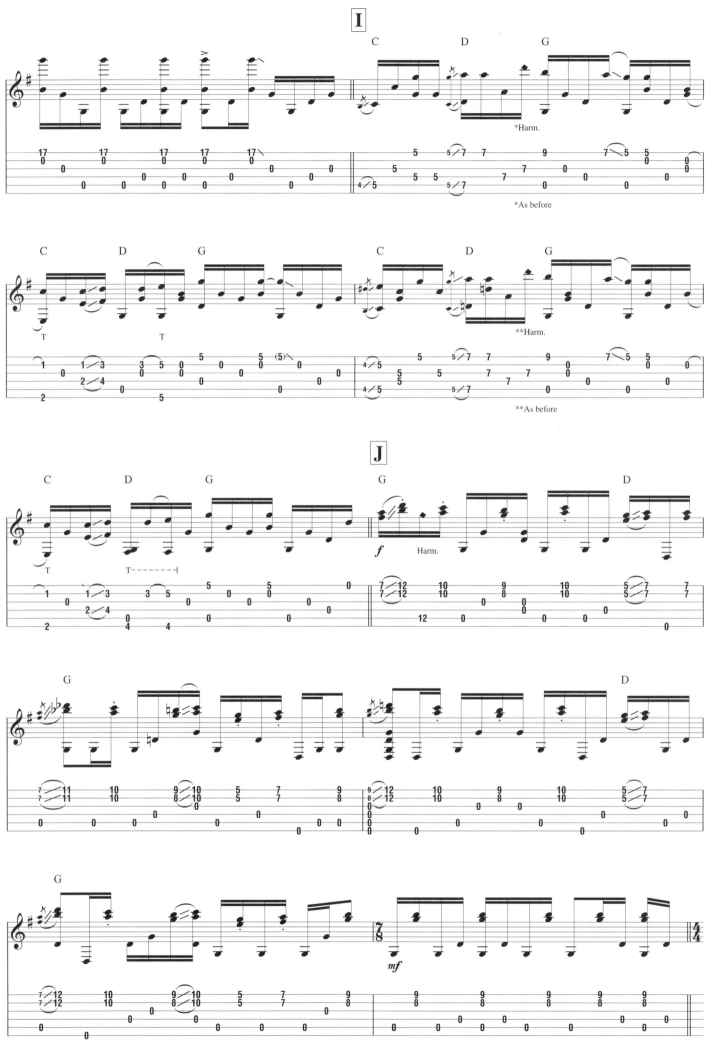

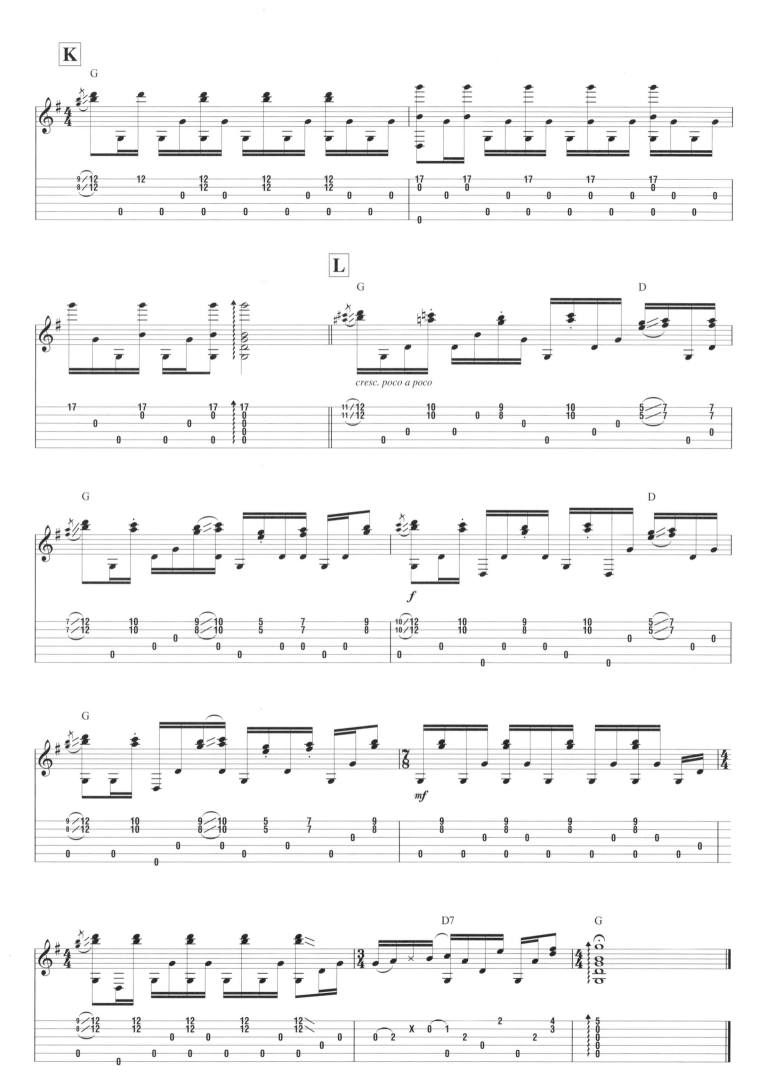

from Michael Hedges - *Pure Michael Hedges*

Layover

Composed by Michael Hedges

Tuning:
(low to high) D-A-C-G-C-E

*Chord symbols reflect implied harmony.

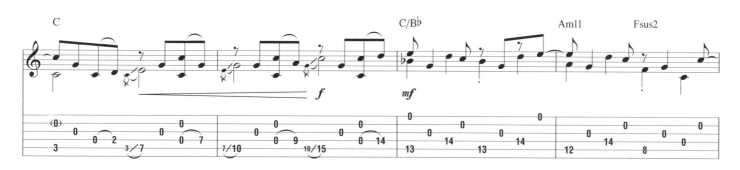

2nd time, Gtr. 1: w/ Fill 1

*Harmonic produced by touching
vibrating strings at the designated frets.

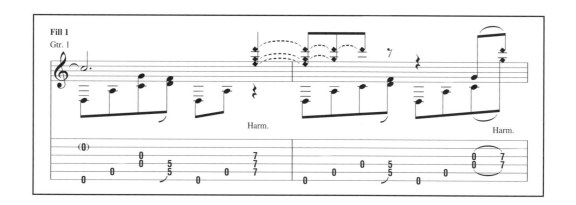

C

*Harm.

*Refers to downstemmed notes only.

**Harm.

**As before

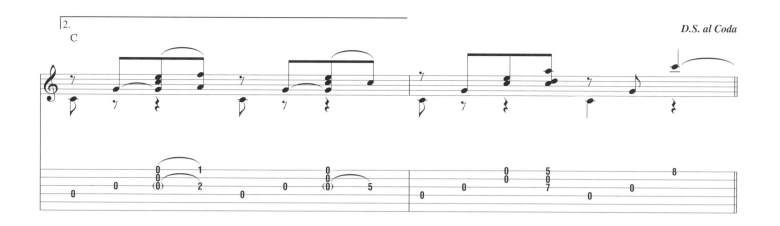

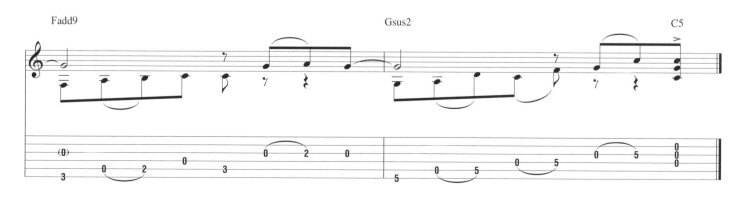

from The Allman Brothers Band - *Eat a Peach*

Little Martha

Written by Duane Allman

Open E tuning:
(low to high) E-B-E-G#-B-E

*Duane Allman **Chord symbols reflect combined harmony.

***Dickey Betts

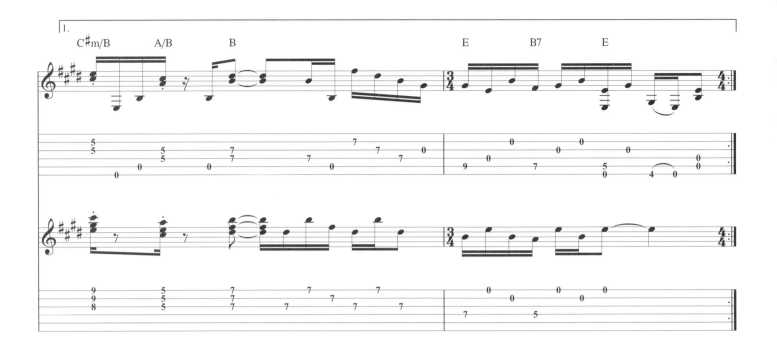

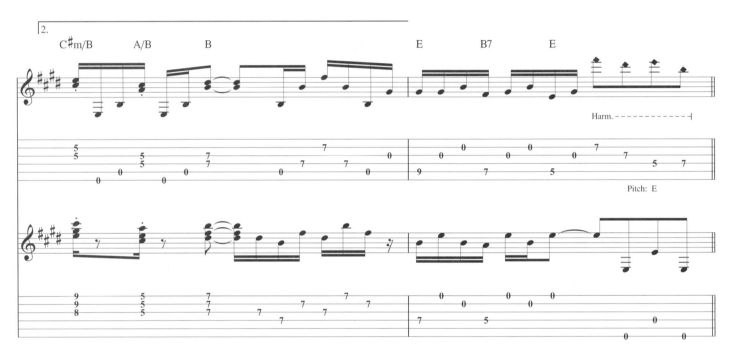

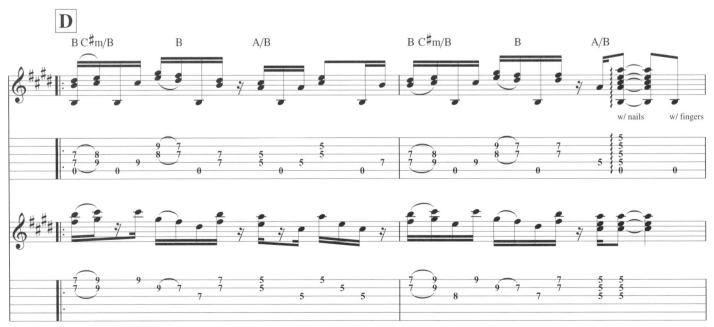

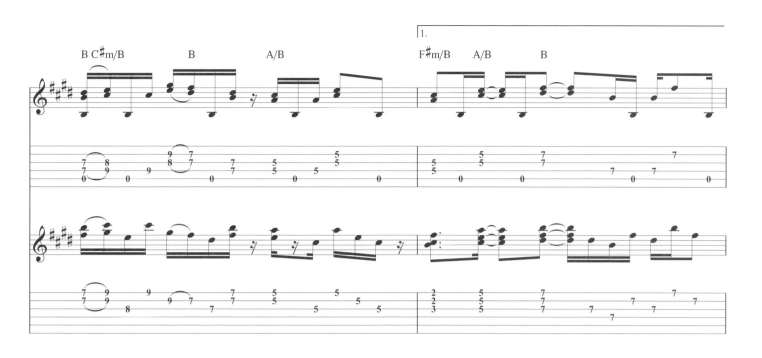

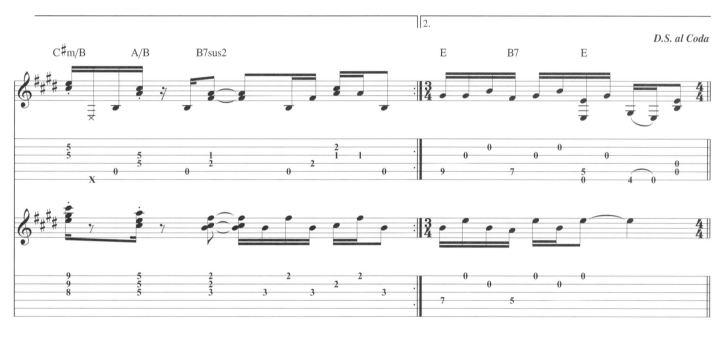

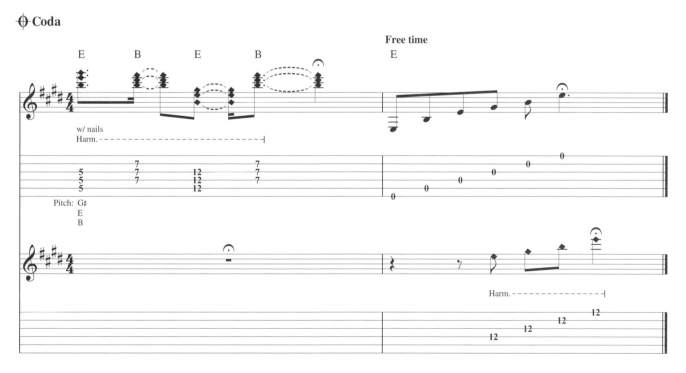

Julia

Words and Music by John Lennon and Paul McCartney

Capo II

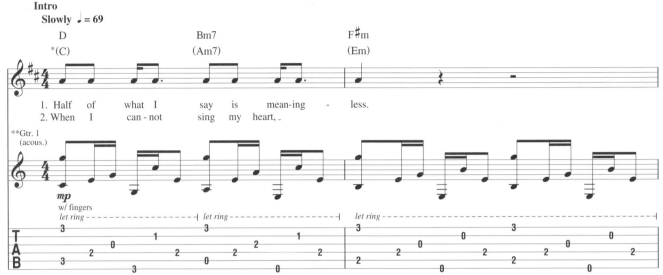

*Symbols in parentheses represent chord names respective to capoed guitar.
Symbols above reflect actual sounding chords. Capoed fret is "0" in tab.
Chord symbols reflect implied harmony.

**John Lennon

***Doubled throughout

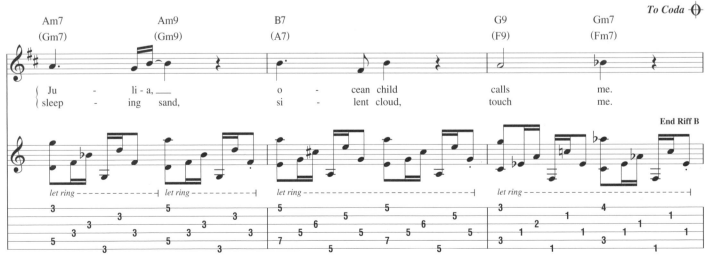

from Tommy Emmanuel - *The Mystery*

Lewis & Clark

By Tommy Emmanuel

Capo II

Free time

*Symbols in parentheses represent chord names respective to capoed guitar.
Symbols above reflect actual sounding chords. Capoed fret is "0" in tab.
Chord symbols reflect implied harmony.

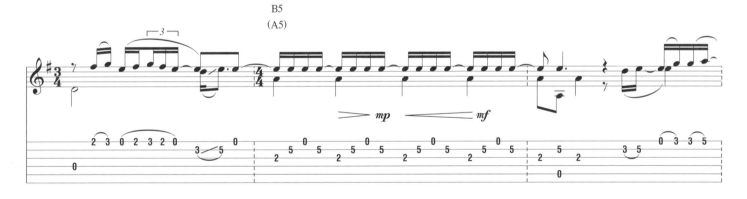

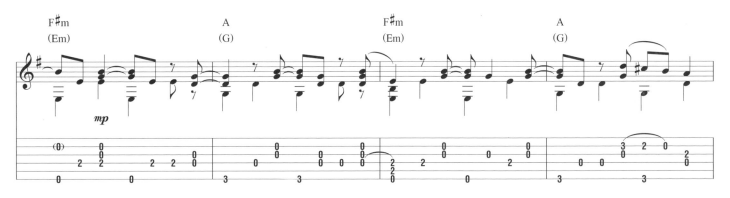

To Coda 2 ⊕

D.S. al Coda 1
(take 2nd ending)

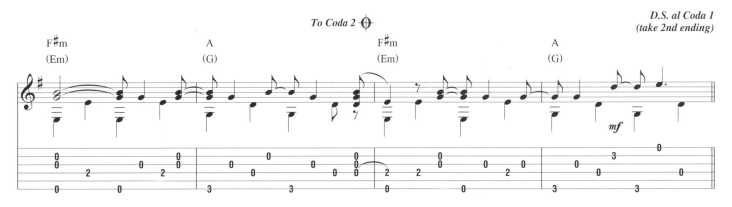

⊕ **Coda 1**

D.S.S. al Coda 2

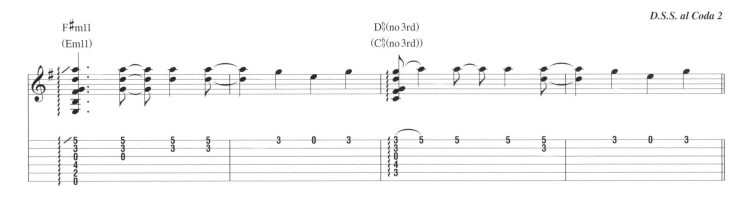

⊕ Coda 2

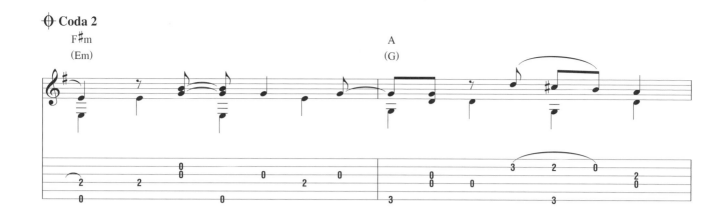

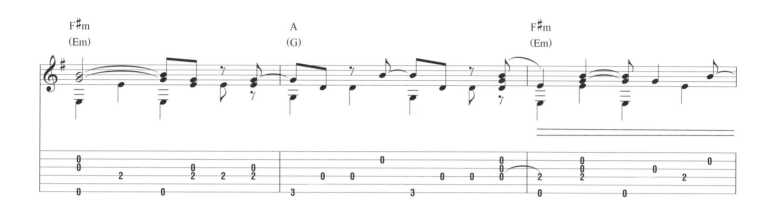

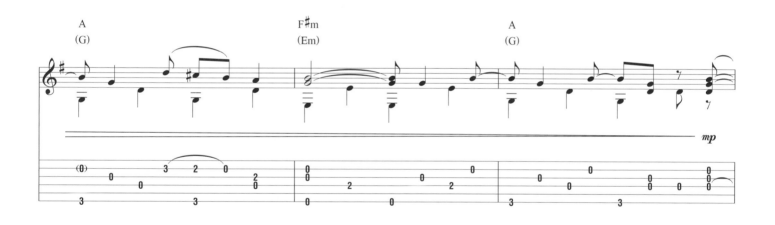

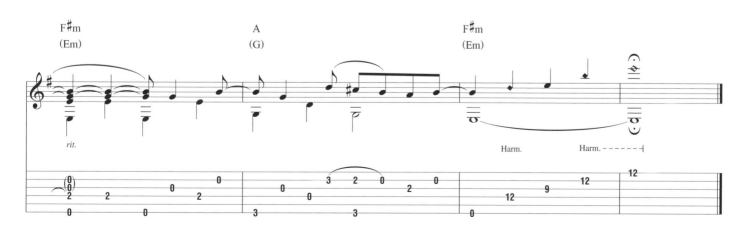

Mister Sandman

Lyric and Music by Pat Ballard

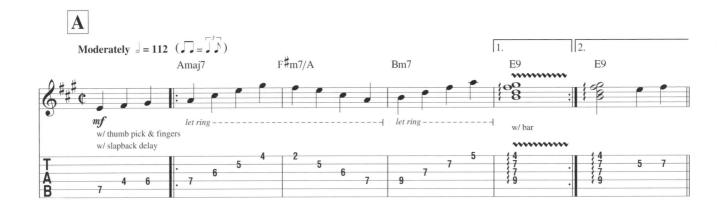

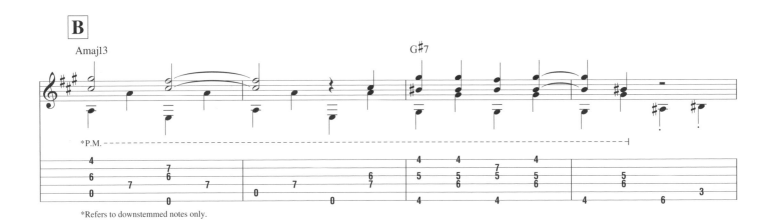

*Refers to downstemmed notes only.

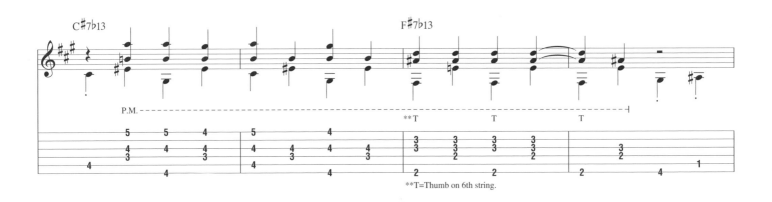

**T=Thumb on 6th string.

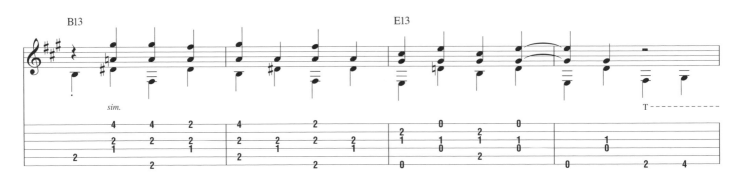

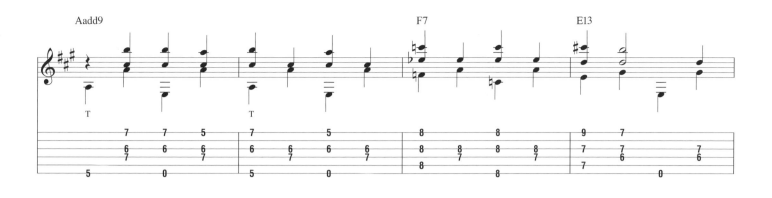

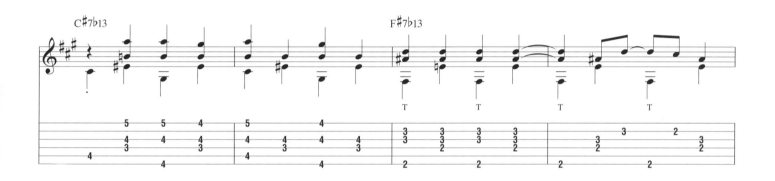

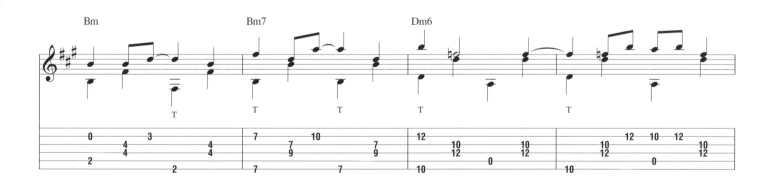

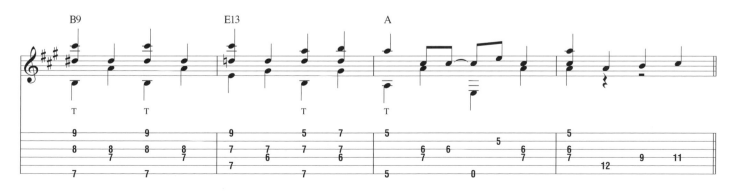

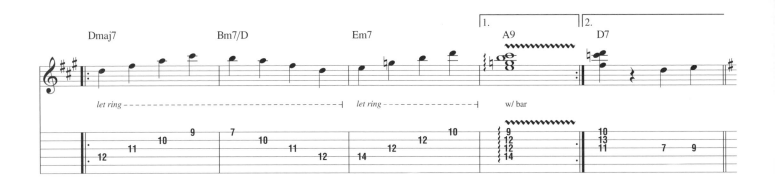

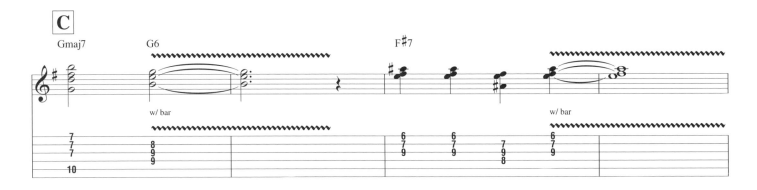

C

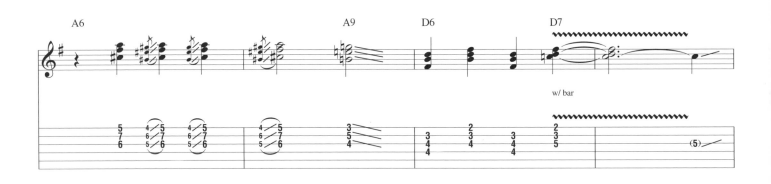

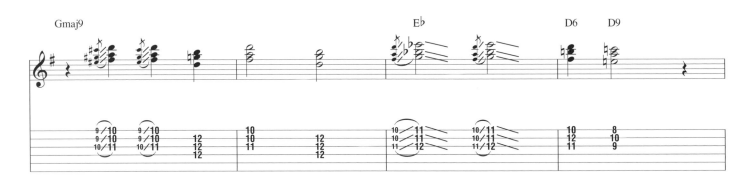

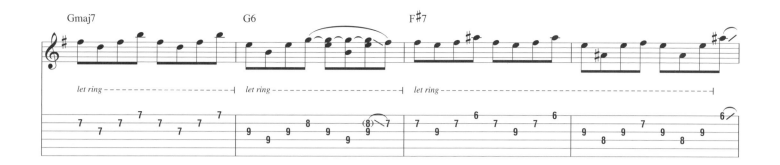

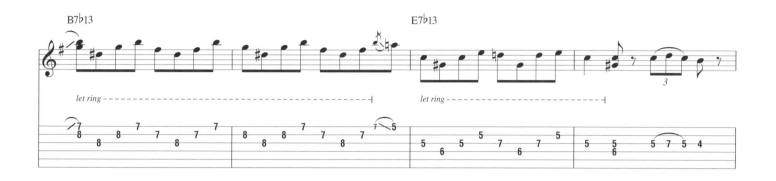

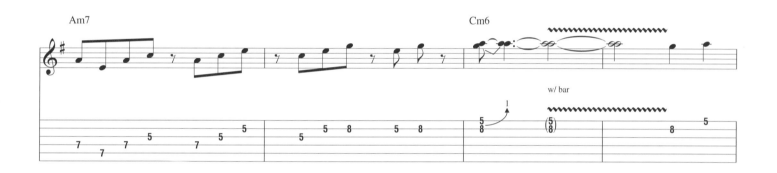

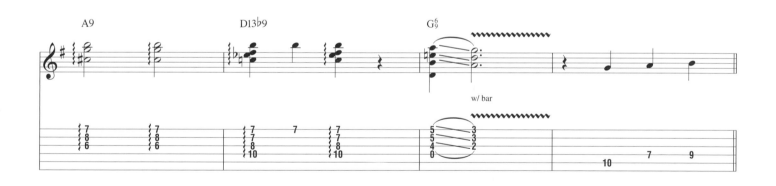

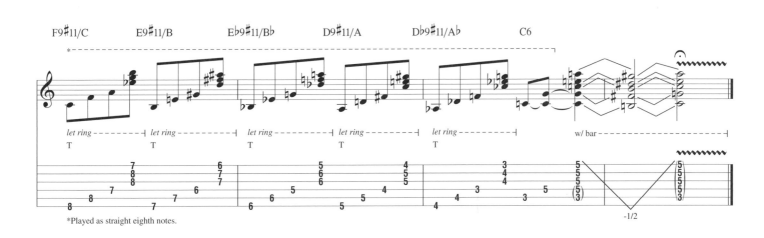

*Played as straight eighth notes.

149

from Leo Kottke - *One Guitar, No Vocals*

Morning Is the Long Way Home

By Leo Kottke

Drop D tuning, down 1/2 step:
(low to high) D♭-A♭-D♭-G♭-B♭-E♭

A

Moderately ♩ = 105

*Chord symbols reflect implied harmony.

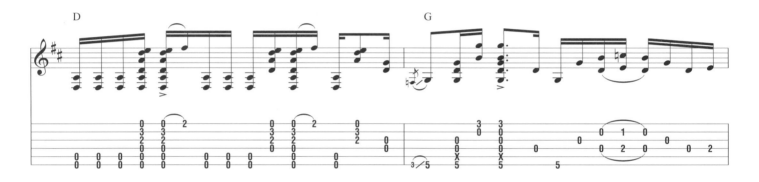

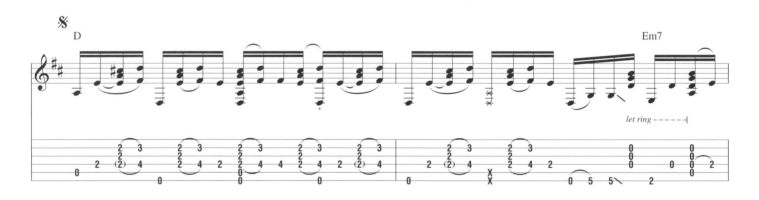

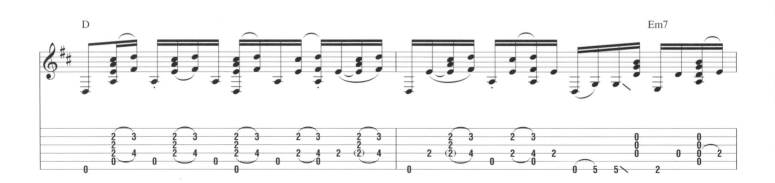

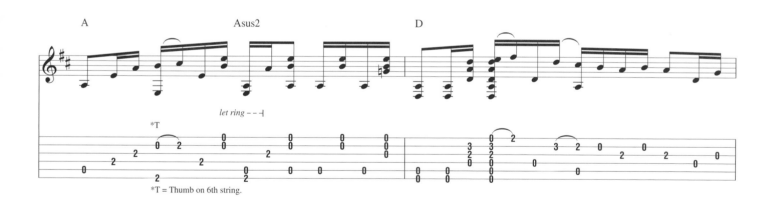

*T = Thumb on 6th string.

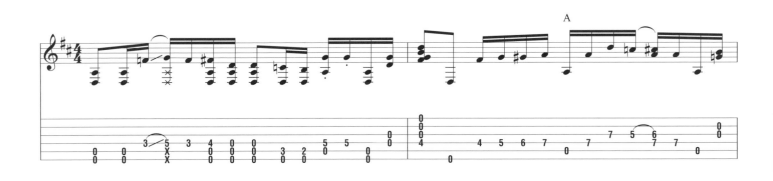

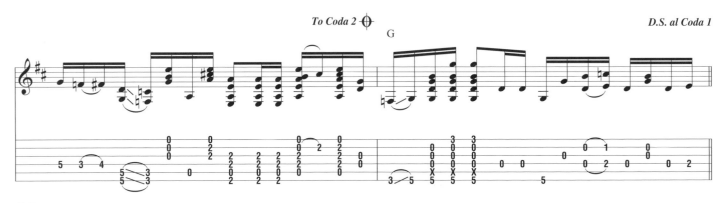

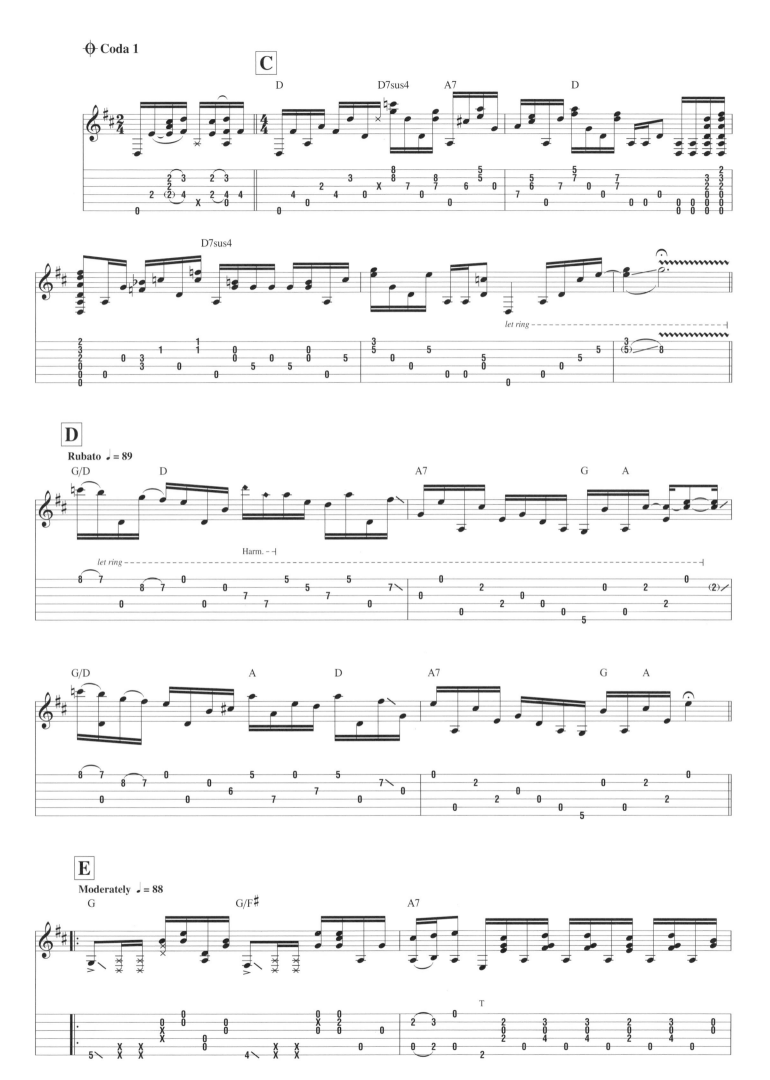

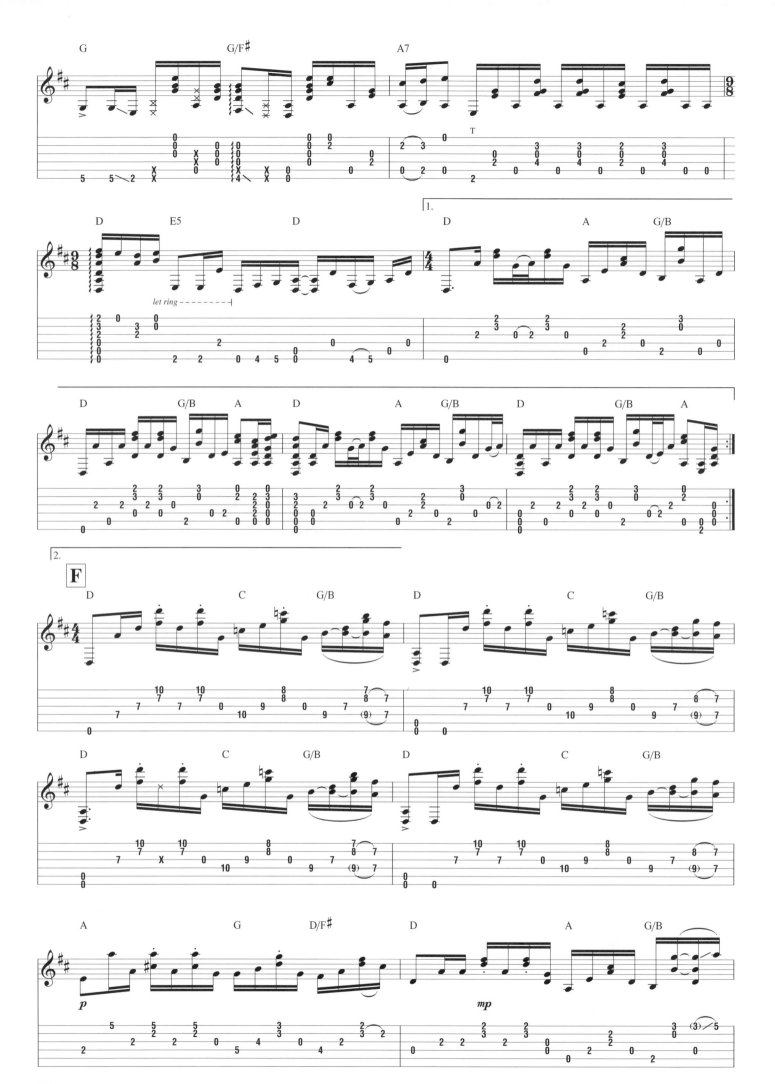

from Eric Johnson - *Ah Via Musicom*

Song for George

By Eric Johnson

Drop D Tuning:
① = D   ④ = D
② = B   ⑤ = A
③ = G   ⑥ = D

Moderately ♩ = 94

Dsus4   D5

NOTE: Play finger style throughout w/ thumb plucking bass part (shown with down stems).

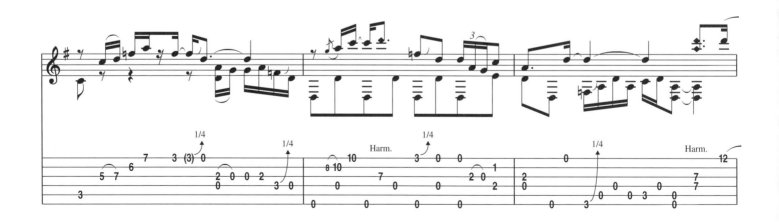

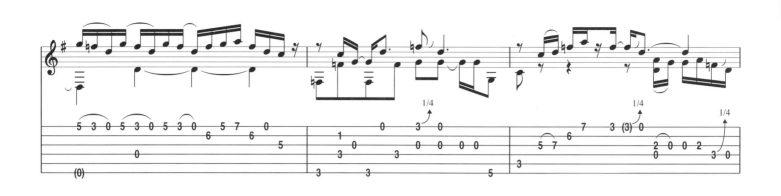

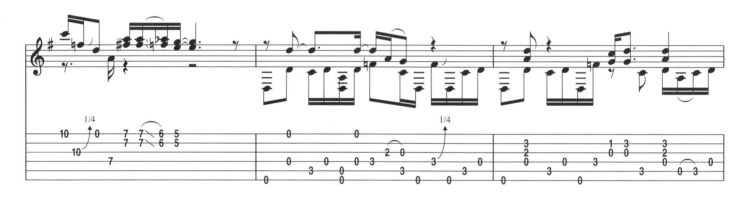

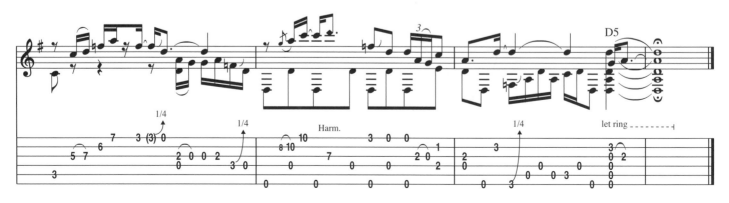

Tears in Heaven

Words and Music by Eric Clapton and Will Jennings

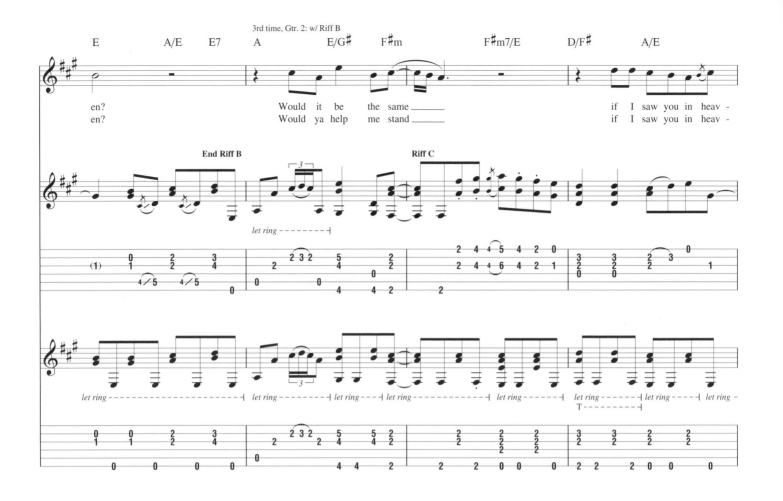

have ya beg - gin', please. Beg - gin' please.

Guitar Solo

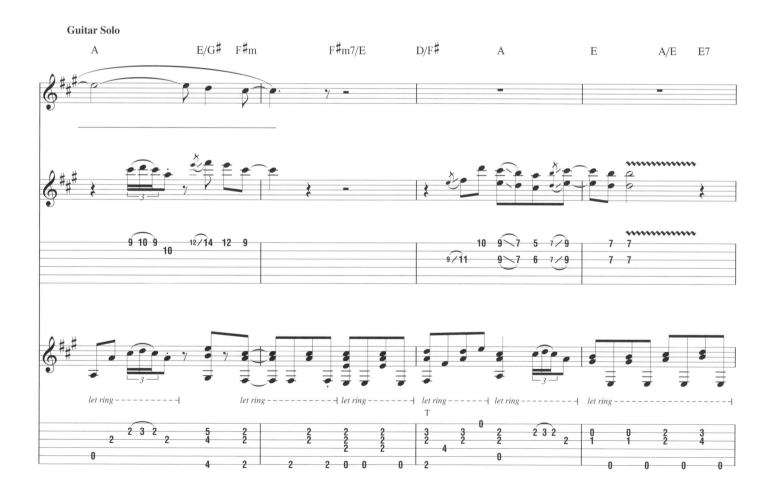

Coda

E7sus4 .... A .... E/G# .... F#m .... F#m7/E

here _ in heav - en.   'Cause _ I

know   I   don't   be - long ___   here _ in heav - en.

*Downstroke

from Jim Croce - *You Don't Mess Around With Jim*

Time in a Bottle

Words and Music by Jim Croce

Gtr. 2: Capo V

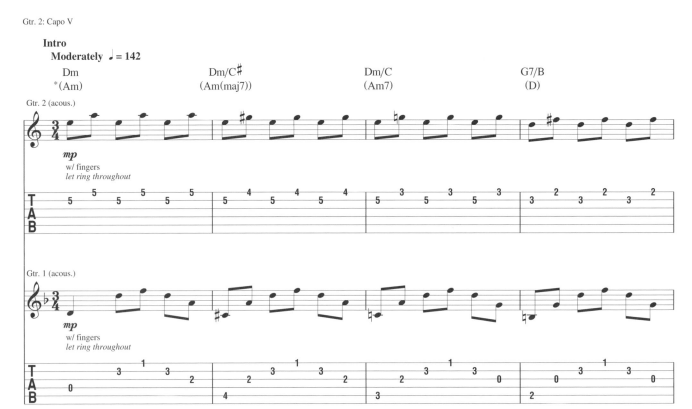

*Symbols in parentheses represent chord names respective to capoed guitar.
Symbols above reflect actual sounding chords. Capoed fret is "0" in tab.
Chord symbols reflect implied harmony.

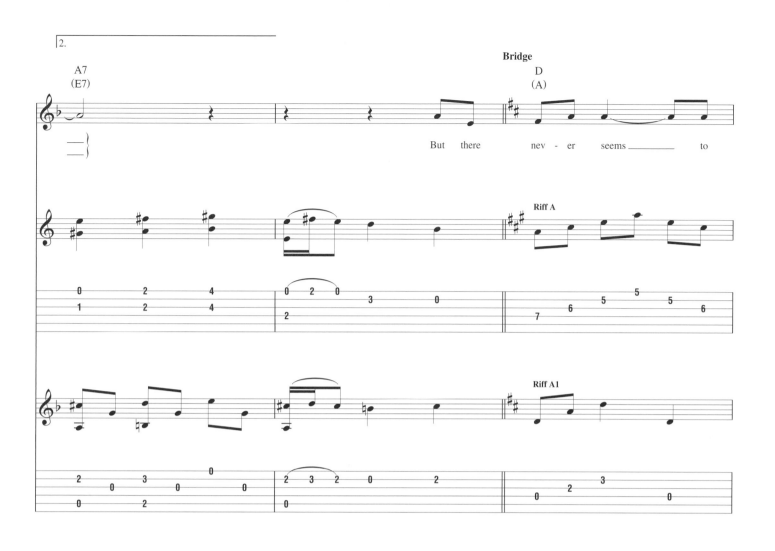

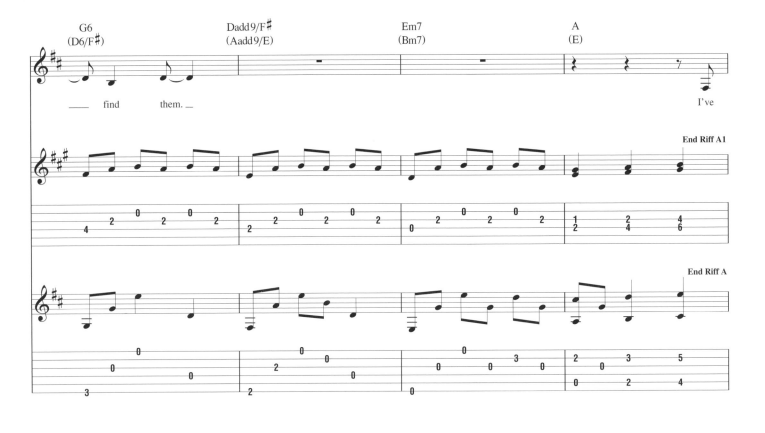

find them. ___   I've

1st time, Gtrs. 1 & 2: w/ Riffs A & A1
2nd time, Gtrs. 1 & 2: w/ Riffs A & A1 (1st 7 meas.)

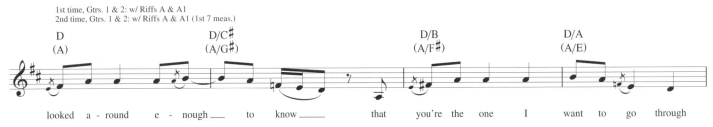

looked a - round e - nough ___ to know ___ that you're the one I want to go through

To Coda ⊕   *D.C. al Coda*
                                                              (take 2nd ending)

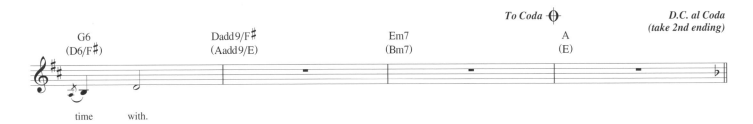

time with.

⊕ **Coda**

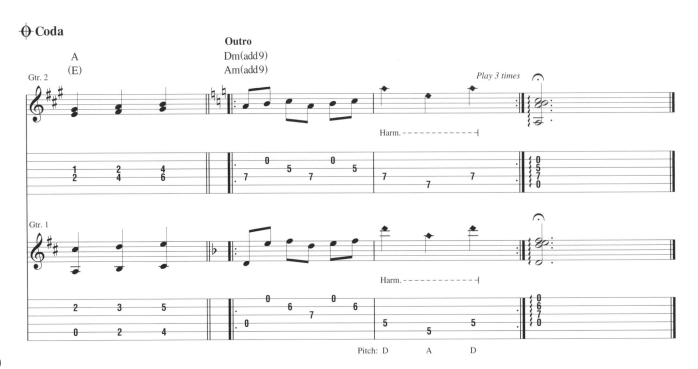

Pitch: D   A   D

Watermelon

By Leo Kottke

Open D tuning, down 1 1/2 steps:
(low to high) B-F#-B-D#-F#-B

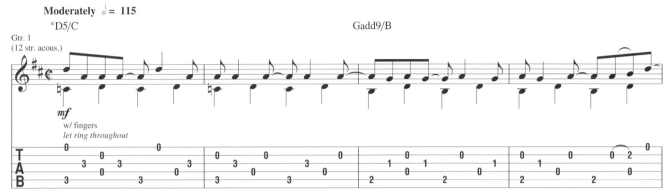

*Chord symbols reflect implied harmony.

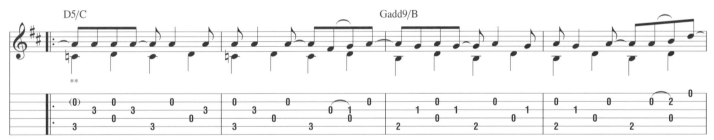

**2nd time, w/o slide.

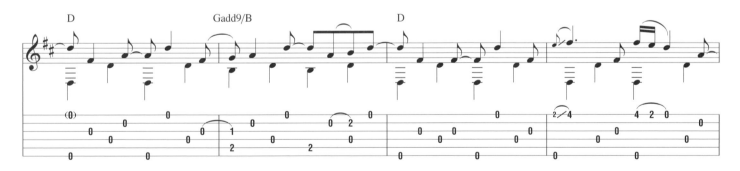

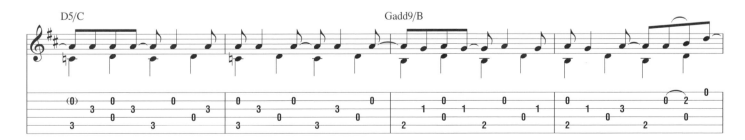

D

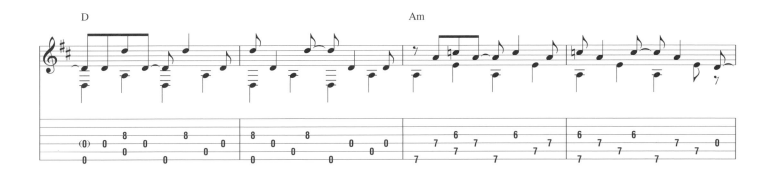

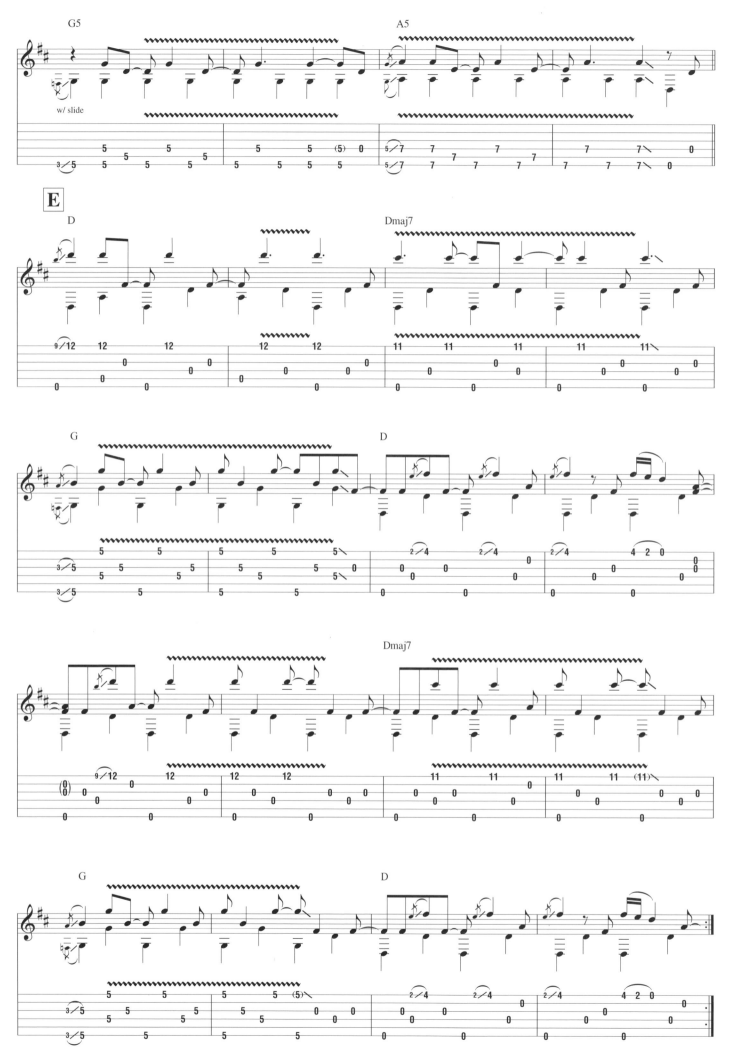

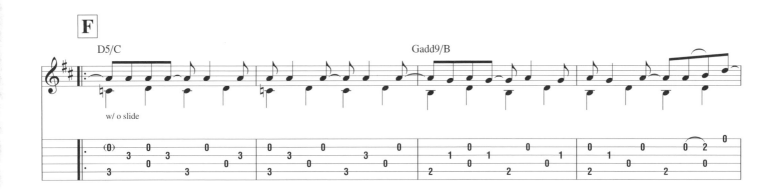

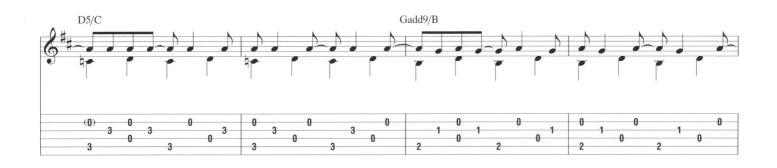

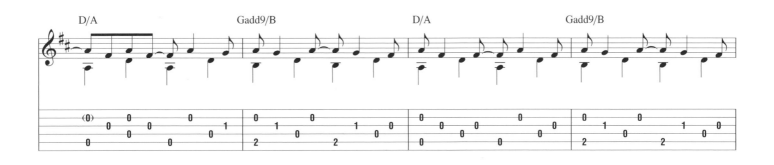

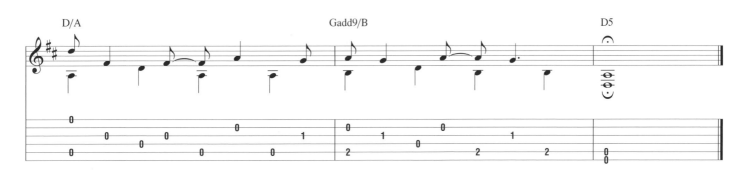

GUITAR NOTATION LEGEND

Guitar music can be notated three different ways: on a *musical staff*, in *tablature*, and in *rhythm slashes*.

RHYTHM SLASHES are written above the staff. Strum chords in the rhythm indicated. Use the chord diagrams found at the top of the first page of the transcription for the appropriate chord voicings. Round noteheads indicate single notes.

THE MUSICAL STAFF shows pitches and rhythms and is divided by bar lines into measures. Pitches are named after the first seven letters of the alphabet.

TABLATURE graphically represents the guitar fingerboard. Each horizontal line represents a string, and each number represents a fret.

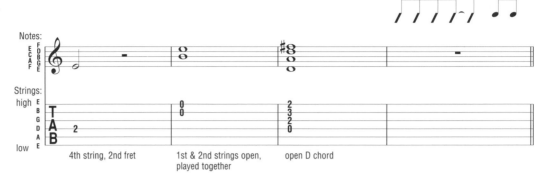

4th string, 2nd fret   1st & 2nd strings open, played together   open D chord

---

HALF-STEP BEND: Strike the note and bend up 1/2 step.

WHOLE-STEP BEND: Strike the note and bend up one step.

GRACE NOTE BEND: Strike the note and immediately bend up as indicated.

SLIGHT (MICROTONE) BEND: Strike the note and bend up 1/4 step.

BEND AND RELEASE: Strike the note and bend up as indicated, then release back to the original note. Only the first note is struck.

PRE-BEND: Bend the note as indicated, then strike it.

VIBRATO: The string is vibrated by rapidly bending and releasing the note with the fretting hand.

WIDE VIBRATO: The pitch is varied to a greater degree by vibrating with the fretting hand.

HAMMER-ON: Strike the first (lower) note with one finger, then sound the higher note (on the same string) with another finger by fretting it without picking.

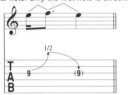

PULL-OFF: Place both fingers on the notes to be sounded. Strike the first note and without picking, pull the finger off to sound the second (lower) note.

LEGATO SLIDE: Strike the first note and then slide the same fret-hand finger up or down to the second note. The second note is not struck.

SHIFT SLIDE: Same as legato slide, except the second note is struck.

TRILL: Very rapidly alternate between the notes indicated by continuously hammering on and pulling off.

TAPPING: Hammer ("tap") the fret indicated with the pick-hand index or middle finger and pull off to the note fretted by the fret hand.

NATURAL HARMONIC: Strike the note while the fret-hand lightly touches the string directly over the fret indicated.

PINCH HARMONIC: The note is fretted normally and a harmonic is produced by adding the edge of the thumb or the tip of the index finger of the pick hand to the normal pick attack.

PICK SCRAPE: The edge of the pick is rubbed down (or up) the string, producing a scratchy sound.

MUFFLED STRINGS: A percussive sound is produced by laying the fret hand across the string(s) without depressing, and striking them with the pick hand.

PALM MUTING: The note is partially muted by the pick hand lightly touching the string(s) just before the bridge.

RAKE: Drag the pick across the strings indicated with a single motion.

TREMOLO PICKING: The note is picked as rapidly and continuously as possible.

VIBRATO BAR DIVE AND RETURN: The pitch of the note or chord is dropped a specified number of steps (in rhythm), then returned to the original pitch.

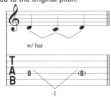

VIBRATO BAR SCOOP: Depress the bar just before striking the note, then quickly release the bar.

VIBRATO BAR DIP: Strike the note and then immediately drop a specified number of steps, then release back to the original pitch.